THE FUTURE OF ADVERTISING, MARKETING AND DIGITAL MEDIA

By

Agustín Medina

Contents

THE FUTURE OF ADVERTISING, MARKETING AND DIGITAL MEDIA 1
    Are you sure you are running a real business when it's not digital? 4
    Antisocial networks 11
    The fan factor in the social networks. 13
    Internet advertising is not yet invented. 16
    The inherent risk of the idea 19

The great writer Arthur C. Clarke thought that;" *Every revolutionary idea seems to evoke three stages of reaction. They may be summed up by the phrases: (1) It's completely impossible. (2) It's possible, but it's not worth doing. (3) I said it was a good idea all along.*" 20
    The dead people of Facebook 21
    The essence of creativity 23
    How about your imagination? 27
    Learn to be creative 29
    Where did talent go? 31
    The MOVER method 33
    Information Overdose 37
    Slaves of Technology 39
    Digital communication 41
    Blue Oceans 42
    The new communication (1) 45

The new communication (2)	48
Three revolutions that "changed" the rules of advertising.	50
Do you also want to be creative?	54
Engagement Marketing	56
The classic marketing techniques is surpassed by the transformation of products into brands.	61
The day the brands died	65
Brand and the brand image	68
How to build a brand	71
A name is not a brand	74
Is anyone really an expert in social networks?	77
MAD MEN	79
The Devalued Lions of Cannes.	83
The basis of advertising	85
Green ads on the highway	88
When the Berlin Wall was decorated with graffiti.	91
Rock and advertising	94
1900 Russian advertising.	98
Have you already tried the Google Glasses?	107
Smartphone: Our sixth damned sense	110
Anonymous beings	112
Internet is a minefield	114
Advertising in ruins	117
Boring creativity, outdated agencies	120
Opportunity for entrepreneurs	122
Learning to follow through.	123
Cholo Simeone, model of leader.	128
The imperfect leadership	131
Speaking about leaders	134
The attitude of the leader in front of the crisis	136
Praise of failure	139
Less is always more	144
Lifehacking: the art of doing nothing	146
Latin America	147
Looking for trends? Go to Japan	149

Are you sure you are running a real business when it's not digital?

Marketing + Sales magazine.

One of the things that have changed the most over the last years is the concept of business management. Traditionally, the common denominator of a company was having a permanent staff, concrete facilities and adherence to a common idea within the business. Take a bank for example; with centralized headquarters in a major city and hundreds of branches in strategic locations throughout, where customers had the certainty that real people were handling their money and careful watchmen safekeeping their investments inside a well-protected area. In today's world, most banks do away with staff and office space to conduct business as usual through digital media.

Internet has allowed millions of people worldwide to use their private homes as workplaces and has helped thousands of companies outsource much of their activities to other companies that service them in other countries thousands of miles away. In Spain, people are used to hear a Latin American voice on the other side of the line responding our requests to help us in any domestic services such as electricity, gas, water or the telephone. That voice comes from another continent where companies have outsourced their call centers with local personnel, thus saving and significantly lowering labor expenses.

This is not exclusive to commodities being transferred to external suppliers; talent and innovation services also perform better and at a lower cost form outside the company. Open Innovation is wreaking havoc not only in the world of communications and advertising production, where it had its beginnings, and many technology oriented companies are looking for talent in these platforms to solve all kinds of problems, from advertising to scientific research for pharmaceutical companies like Eli Lilly, the American manufacturer of the famous as Prozac and Cialis.

It is a question of taking advantage of the natural talent of millions of anonymous people, professional or not, that accept the challenge to work from their homes to compete on almost any field.

The bidding company places certain requirements on the platform and offers monetary remuneration to the winner of the bid. Henceforth, the company starts receiving proposals from the remotest corners of the globe, often exceeding all expectations. Because talent moves in infinite numbers throughout the network, proof of this are the thousands of spectacular videos posted on YouTube every day.

Using the net to find talent or to sell products or services anywhere in the world is just two among many uses new technologies can bring to your business. In the World of today, to consider that a company is really in the XXI Century, it's not enough to practice e-commerce or having a website and a more or less active presence in different social networks, it also has to be engaged in developing new technologies, and in order to benefit from the immense untapped opportunities in the system, it is necessary to go even further, you really have to take the big conceptual leap to understand that -"digital"- is not a temporary phenomenon that affects specific areas of your company, it is a revolution that is not only here to stay, but it also requires a drastic change of strategy in all the business levels.

Many companies still play the love me, love me not game with the daisy to decide whether it's convenient or not to use a social media background and having an online presence larger that a mere testimony of modernity but rather, they still think that the new technologies are only affecting Marketing and Communications departments, because of their more direct relationship with its customers, while other areas of the company are foreign to these "modernity". Certainly, these companies see the wave of progress running over their heads, and time is running out before suffocating in the waters of indecision.

Today, digital is not only an option for communications between companies and their customers or a new sales channel for their products. The digital technology, as a whole, must be present in all areas of the company as well as in all relations with its stakeholders, so that the DNA of any company with projections for the future can be an essential part of it. This should permeate all business strategy and should be learned by all staff as a priority to be considered in all internal and external decision-making.

Each person on the team must understand that technological tools go far beyond the day-to-day use of computers, it is necessary to create awareness that the customer is now the focus of all processes and that customer relations is about being present in all the important moments of their lives, thus making our brand a true companion to his or her journey.

This can only be achieved if we understand that the digital world is already inherent in all human experiences, both personal and professional, and in their role as consumers of products or services. It is only then that we can level the playing field to benefit both parties involved to ensure that our business will continue moving into future as a real business.

Blog Interview for More Mobility

Where is the border between communication and marketing?

Borders are blurred because of the shift in relevance the market once had throughout the twentieth century, and in today's world the consumer is king. The power has changed hands; today real power lays in communication with the consumer, managed by marketing rules. In fact, some business schools provide a masters degree for Marcom, which is an acronym for Marketing and Communication. I believe that this new interest in training professionals' combining the two disciplines is evident proof that the lines have been crossed.

Where is creativity standing? Are the new tools helping or are they becoming a hindrance?
There is no doubt in my mind that these new tools enable creativity because they afford new models of expression. What happens is that creativity is not always associated to the professional areas; this can be verified with the many videos uploaded on YouTube each day, spontaneous creativity and talent from ordinary people far exceeds the output of the average communications professional.

Are BBDD, CRM and RRSS currently the three pillars of marketing?
Tools have always been just that, tools, but today they have become more effective playing an important role to identify opportunities, but nevertheless, it is important to handle them with good judgment to plan an intelligent strategy to get the best out of it, provided be handled by a professional.

It seems that some brands achieve customer loyalty through social networks, but can this be transformed?
I have many doubts that the relationship between customers and brands via social networks will translate into sales. I think networks are another element to foster empathy with brands, but they build a long-term brand relationship with the image rather than for short-term sales.

Is it easier or more difficult to reach consumers given the large amount of media deployed and consolidated in recent years?
It is easier to address micromarketing processes to reach very specific targets. As for the big targets, they are still in the hands of the mainstream media like television and radio, they still successfully communicate with large audiences.

It is well known that "the consumer is the king" What can brands do to seduce him to the wide range of messages they receive each day?
There are a few secrets: smart strategies, brilliant communication, honesty, transparency and creativity in all processes.

"Branded Content" is increasingly widespread, but is only available to the big brands. Can SMEs also use this strategy?
I believe that Branded Content is the advertising of the future; there are great examples of what can be done with imagination and very limited resources to make it available for any brand, large or small.
And it can also develop all kinds of tools; it is not limited to the new digital media.

In your predictions for 2015 you mention the Gamification? You don't you see a future in it?
I do not think that Gamification in itself is an authority as a trend; I believe it's an activity that would be more fitted for temporary promotional areas, to match the strategic focus of the company.

Antisocial networks

Recently, in an article in "El País Semanal" magazine, Karelia Vázquez mentioned antisocial networking as an example of how people are fed up by being constantly connected and sharing his or her life with everyone through a social network. They're tired of being exposed to the wandering eyes of others and are also fed up with being dependent to the indecent exposure of their daily routine.

It's a clear love-hate relationship, but the use of any networks is voluntary and theoretically created to satisfy the desire to relate to others; but this also fosters fatigue and unwillingness, due to the fact of having become almost an obligation that requires many hours in front of the many different screens.

According Karelia Vázquez, this network dependence has important consequences to many people:

1) It's overwhelming to be constantly approached by unexpected and intrusive friends.

2) This excessive interaction disperses us and affects our memory and concentration and it is also wearisome to be judged by others.

3) It tempts us to invent our reality and create a more flattering image of ourselves.

4) There is a risk of depression for feeling excluded or by comparing the fascinating social and professional lives of others with your own.

5) There is a pressure to keep pace and presence not necessarily comfortable for all users.

6) The risk of obsessive behaviors is rampart.

7) Sentimental breakups are longer and more painful, because the life of the ex-partner is constantly showcased.

As a result of this conventional glut network situation, many people are suffering and a multitude of "antisocial networks" have emerged, some of them very interesting and useful like Unbaby.me, borne from Facebook's inexhaustible stream of baby pictures uploaded by their proud parents. There is also Cloak, an app that locates your contacts and gives you the opportunity to avoid crossing into them.

Antisocial networks are popular and are here to stay; they have become an antidote to the unstoppable emergence of other networks that attempt to fill almost all areas of our already battered privacy.

The fan factor in the social networks.

Recently we have seen a self-promotion campaign of Canal Plus television, where 300 fans of the series Game of Thrones were invited by the network to participate as extras on the show.

The participation of fans in brand advertising is a new phenomenon caused in part, no doubt, by the great influence of social networks in the daily communication between companies and customers. The Canal Plus case has an important precedent with the English chocolate Wixpa, by Cadbury Schweppes.

In 2003 Cadbury decided to stop making Wixpa due to low demand. But five years later, in 2008, an executive of the company found a Facebook page where 20,000 fans of the brand were asking Cadbury to bring back Wixpa into the market.

The executive thought that if there were 20,000 spontaneous applicants, perhaps it was worth the try to harness their enthusiasm and infect many more and bring back the chocolate supported by a large advertising campaign on television.

They began by activating their Facebook page inviting fans to try the new Wixpa for free, this time Wixpa came back by popular demand. They ended up with a big campaign on television using 300 fans (coincidentally the same number as those used by Canal Plus), using the slogan "For the love of Wixpa", in the campaign.

At present, the Wixpa Facebook page has more than two million fans and is the best selling chocolate bar in the UK, with annual sales of over one hundred million pounds.

It seems that using the fans for brand advertising can be quite profitable sometimes.

Internet advertising is not yet invented.

I belong to the creative television generation. When I started my career as a copywriter, television was already the king of the media. However, the brightest and most respected senior creative of the agencies back then, were only creative in print media.

Copywriters wrote long and literary texts for newspapers and magazines, but television was an exclusive field for the producer, he wrote the scripts, hired production companies and supervised the entire process. In McCann, where I worked, this producer was a real genius from Australia named Frank Boss.

Several years went by until the new generation of copywriters and art directors took over from the old advertising men and started to take a bite out of TV spots, my first intervention on this new landscape was in the Gillette GII campaign, played by actor Paco Rabal and filmed in 1972.

Some of the old long text writers adapted more or less well to the 20 seconds television texts, but most were left behind, they could not understand the new media and chose not to resign in favor of the charm of their beautiful literary texts.

Today the same things are happening, the great creative men of my generation and the next are still active and occupying places of privilege in their respective agencies. Owners, partners, or senior leaders thereof still have the power in advertising and like me, are creative for television. They love the environment and scope of television advertisements; they love being the sole authors of the pieces they produce, and adore to collect personal rewards festivals worldwide.

They do not want to learn the codes of new technologies and do not want to be part of an anonymous group of people making viral YouTube videos or promotions on Facebook and other social networks. In fact, they hold on to their television spots waiting for early retirement to then hand it all to the new generations.

They seem to think that the Internet is for young people and as a consequence their agencies have resisted entering the new media until it has become an inevitable move. Moreover, advertising has always been a conservative force and has always resisted, like a scalded cat, everything even before the digital phenomenon came into play enthusiastically shelving their creativity. In fact, there is more spontaneous and amateur creativity online than in all advertising the agencies in the world, you can attest to that by simply watching the thousands of videos that regular people upload on YouTube every day.

The Internet Company that brings more advertising money today is definitely Google Ad-words that, as its name suggests, is only for classified advertising, and there is nothing really new or revolutionary from a creative point of view, even their banners, in their different versions, are nothing but typical Skirt Press. Moreover, their effectiveness has declined from 5% in the early days to a mere 0.5%.

There are also videos on conventional television formats with less production money uploaded on social networks platforms, hoping to become viral, a bestseller desired by all.

I have the impression that less evolved forms of advertising and old creative agencies of today, just like the old copywriters, are always the ones who are not really interested in the world of the Internet, and think that the new digital advertising is bereft of talent. So I state; "Internet advertising has not yet been invented". It will be necessary that a new generation, familiar with the new technologies, harness the power of advertising to give that welcoming transcendent step with creativity and enthusiasm in all new media.

The inherent risk of the idea

Mark Twain said that *a person with a new idea is a crank until the idea succeeds*. Nothing could be truer. New ideas, when they are really new, involve risk and revolution, two concepts that has always scared everybody.

Edison said a hundred of times that the bulb was a stupid invention, and fifteen publishers rejected the first manuscript of J.K. Rowling, creator of Harry Potter, because none wanted to take the risk of printing such an extensive book dedicated to an infantile and juvenile audience.

John Kennedy Toole was also a reject with his novel "A Confederacy of Dunces" by all US publishers, he could not swallow rejection and committed suicide at 32 immersed in frustration and disappointment, but his mother kept sending the manuscript everywhere until it was published and became one of the leaders of the best American literature of the twentieth century.

Crank or genius, the creators of new ideas are, one way or the other, always depending on the whimsical decisions of fate and being in the right place at the right time, or with the character to resist all setbacks, negativity and indolence without ever throwing the towel. These are some of the keys to achieve success with your ideas.

The great writer Arthur C. Clarke thought that;" *Every revolutionary idea seems to evoke three stages of reaction. They may be summed up by the phrases: (1) It's completely impossible. (2) It's possible, but it's not worth doing. (3) I said it was a good idea all along."*

When you succeed everyone agrees to the greatness of your idea, but before that, very few dared to bet on it. Only if you have mustered the courage to move forward when assuming all the risks because, as Oscar Wilde said: "An idea that is not dangerous is unworthy of being called an idea at all".

The dead people of Facebook

According to a study by the CIA, every day around 154,000 people die in the world making it a total of 56.21 million deaths a year. Given that one in seven inhabitants has a profile on Facebook, we could deduce that out of the 1,000 million users of this network, around 8 million pass to a better life every year.

I've always wondered if the profile of the deceased would still be working after their passing, and if Facebook would use those profiles as useful contacts when selling their ads. That is, when you put an ad on Facebook and accurately define your target group, you could also be buying the corpses of many potential buyers of your product in the selling package of possible contacts.

It is clear to me that the deceased will not remove his or her profile on all social networks, nor is it likely to be done by their relatives or their closest inter alia friends, because to delete a profile without the person concerned is not an easy task.

Not only are there thousands of inert profiles on Facebook and other social networks, but also many of those profiles are apparently still active after their deaths. I have just discovered a trend in the United States to use Facebook pages as a kind of graveyards that one can go to interact with their deceased relatives or friends.

It seems that many people prefer to go on Facebook rather than to the cemetery. And it has a certain logic; instead of praying to the deceased or talk to him in front a cold tombstone, it is closer to home to do so in their live Facebook page, where you can find his or her photos, comments, friends, etc. where the deceased is still somehow present.

We can continue writing to the departed with the same enthusiasm with which we did when he or she was alive, and with the illusion that he remains with us and from one moment to another we will receive a direct message from beyond.

Wilma Jones is a living example of this new relationship with the dead. She past away some time ago, but their relatives and friends keep sending messages and sharing with her all kinds of news through her Facebook page. And probably when we place an ad in the network and our target is defined with any of the characteristics that matched with Wilma when she was alive, we are not also giving her an advertising message and in this case, it is clear that it will be money thrown away, or rather, buried in a tomb.

The essence of creativity

Creativity is basically inventing something new based on something already known. Nothing comes from nothing, we just play over and over again with the clay of ideas to create new ideas, which are always ever-new versions of old things.

In order to create you must have the daring to free associate things that in principle were believed to be impossible to be together. We must be able to give imagination a leap over logic thought and search in the depths of our brain for that spark that will tear to pieces any logical reasoning and enable us to find new and unexpected ways.

Chema Madoz is a photographer from Madrid who plays with imagination by associating different objects giving birth to a new object, a conceptual creation that gives personality to his photographic works.

Finding associations that are beyond logic is the essence of creativity, a very simple concept to explain and understand, but very difficult to execute. If you want to be creative, just try a thousand times.

How about your imagination?

Our brain stores in a bundle all experiences, but we have a limited capacity to manage them and to solve problems with what we can actually remember. What we can remember is just the top of the iceberg of our knowledge, however, the unconscious holds the key to our creative mind.

Handling all the information we store in our brain is an impossible task for the logical mind alone, we need to use our imagination to reach the depths of the unconscious. Imagination is beyond logic and allows us to combine the use of our knowledge to reach the creative act and the discovery of ideas.

All thinkers, philosophers, mathematicians and artists who defined their own creative process, agree on the following:

- Approach the problem.
- Analysis.
- Incubation.
- Inspiration.
- Birth of the Idea

In these all this steps, logic and imagination and conscious and unconscious knowledge are perfectly combined to the way to the birth of an idea. And that's something that can be learned and exercised.

In the marketing world, today more than ever, we need to learn to exercise our creativity because innovation is the key for the development of any company. We must be able to invent everything every day, breaking old patterns and developing new proposals in all areas, from design to marketing strategies.

We must establish guidelines for innovation in our daily work, always keeping our eyes on the goal, learning from everything and everyone, working with passion and daring to face the unknown, because creativity is always born out of risk.

Learn to be creative

Humans are slaves to routine and experience and our creativity is hampered by the rotten habit to search for the correct answers and to platitudes. Albert Einstein said that "imagination is more important than knowledge", a statement that demonstrates that accumulated knowledge isn't necessarily that much of help if we are not able to also develop our imagination to use knowledge in an effective manner.

We all come into the world with a spontaneous creative baggage that, in theory, would allow us to face everything from our own single and different perspective from that of other human beings and therefore, capable to carry out a processes of continuous innovation in all our acts. But society in its effort to integrate the whole teaches rules of conduct and similar behaviors, which slowly undermines our ability to be different by imposing patterns of common experience and shared routines. It would seem that the individual and society were two opposing concepts, but society advances only by the creative force of individuals, so it is very important to develop their creative potential.

To adopt a creative attitude we must begin by assuming that everything is a matter of perspective and that things can be or appear different depending on our particular angle.

There are three key concepts to develop creativity:

- Do not rely solely on experience.

- Do not admit anything as unique and definitive.

- Develop your imagination through the constant production of associations.

Following these rules with the awareness that creativity is an attitude, we can develop our creativity to levels we could have never imagined.

Where did talent go?

I have been advertising creative all my professional life, and ever since I accepted to be the creative director of Norman Craig & Kummel, I have also been evaluating the talent of other people. I was also part of the jury in advertising festivals around the world 31 times, including 10 as jury president.

I think that my experience as an observer of talent gives me ground to say that these moments are probably the saddest in the history of advertising in our country. The list of winners of the most important advertising awards only reinforces my view.

We can verify this by merely watching prime time television or a battery of promotional in the social networks to see that talent is absent. Naturally there is always a spark that shines by itself, but that beam fails to conceal the tremendous mediocrity of the whole. It can be said that there is more spontaneous talent on YouTube that in all of the advertising industry.

The explanation for this situation probably has to do with many factors:

a) The economic crisis cannot pay for real talent.
b) Overpopulation of juniors and trainees in advertising agencies,

c) A negative situation of the industry, confusion by the new media, etc.

The truth is that in order for advertising to work, it has to be bright and with the ability to seduce the public to the point that they wish to see it, share it and enjoy it. When we love advertising we see ads over and over again, no matter if those ads interrupt our favorite show. Indeed, viewers in the decades of the 80s and 90s stated that they liked enjoyed advertisements over television programs.

Today people hate those endless blocks of commercials interrupting our leisure time, and he disgusting advertising of today not only bore us, but also pursue us wherever we go. The classic structure of the mainstream media has been broken into pieces and ads enter to the depths of our intimacy through the new media.

Internet knows everything about us thanks to the information we give every time we use Google, or in our social networking profiles. This information is viciously used every time you connect to the network.

I think this issue is not irreversible and today's companies leaving to other more lucrative areas will return to advertising again. I hope in the future we can come back to a more haunting advertising, rather than a pursuing nightmare.

The MOVER method

In my book "Bye, bye, marketing" I developed a method to develop collective awareness of the importance of change and innovation in all processes, and the necessary involvement of all staff to achieve all business objectives.

Then I show a summary of the essentials of the method.

Make others become Aware: Put into the minds of all employees the importance of change and innovation, making them see their professional life and that the future of the company depends on those principles.

Objectives: It is important that the company determines collective goals of change in all areas.

Strategic **V**ision: Making plans for an ongoing research to assess the chances of success of all the implemented projects.

Execution: Once the most interesting projects are defined, execute them without reservations.

Resistances: Penalizing the resistances and encouraging the complete involvement of people is the best guarantee for success.

Information Overdose

I eat breakfast with political information, a snack with war reporters who tell me atrocities, lunch with the Middle East conflicts and dinner with television series about crimes and lawyers. Additionally, I am bombarded with hundreds of emails, tweets and messages from all my Facebook friends, Pinterest, Google + and LinkedIn.

The truth is that I do not have the time to process all daily information and I fear I'm missing the most essential things on the side of the road and cannot really understand all of the issues because I do not have time to delve into each one of them.

I imagine the same thing happens to almost everyone, however I hear people speak ex-cathedra about all these matters, dishing out dogmatic opinions without the slightest embarrassment.

They merely adjust to a new public opinion defending their positions, often based on superficial information and here say. They are giving shape to a new public and it fills me with contempt. There are talks of finishing with the old system and building a new order better for everyone, but I am full of doubts because I do not think the cultural foundations for the future of the new generations are sufficiently strong.

I think we need to think well and that we must learn to listen and think deeply before issuing categorical judgments and above all, I believe we must learn to separate the wheat from the chaff before making decisions and undertake actions that sometimes are irreversible.

Slaves of Technology

"Human does not value things by themselves but through images that he or she can make out of them, in fact they know to select images from the television and makes judgments with the words he or she hears from the mouth of a commentator. The world has become larger and wider and the mass media, although apparently is there to make things closer, they actually distance each other because they make us believe that everything is within our reach and that we can embrace it all and assimilate it all. They provide a botcher culture, superficial and ambiguous. They teach us the art of knowing everything by not knowing anything.

A medieval man living in a remote village had a small, tiny but familiar and known world. He knew the smell of the land and the weight of each stone with which he built his house, knew every neighbor, every pet, every house, every tree and every path. And though their world was very small, they were closer than us to the universe. His view of things had a pulse, a life, a feeling and a smell, whereas our senses have been atrophied by the press and the cathode rays from the television".

I wrote those lines in an article for the Communication journal in June 1975. Today, 38 years later, I think they are more relevant than ever because the media noise from back then is joined by all the information to form a tsunami and then the Internet complicated everything.

We have at our disposal all the information possible but our time to assimilate it has increasingly declined; we are reducing our culture to clichés shared by the masses. Millions of contents fly over our heads, barely scratching our brains without penetrating it.

We have learned to handle a few technological tools that give us a sense of power over everything, but in reality we are just slaves of that same technology, a kind of magic wand that brings us things without touching them, feeling them and assimilating them, because their magic is too fast for our limited ability to manage our own time.

Digital communication

I have 14,500 followers on Twitter (@agustin13) and write several tweets every day, normally a tweet remains no more than a minute and a half on my computer screen. Early in the morning during peak time, this average drops to about 30 seconds in which my 14,500 followers read the information I send them, which means that only those who are connected and attentive during those 30 seconds can read my message.

The others have to check every day on my profile and see the latest tweets to catch up. Obviously, this requires an effort of loyalty and I'm guessing that about 2% or 3% of my followers' possess.
This Twitter example, given the time frame, is also applicable to other social networks.

Then there is the content. On YouTube for example, people upload one hour of video every second and there are more than 700 million web pages available to us right now. Digital noise is deafening, not to mention the monumental digital garbage filling those millions of pages, making it almost impossible to escape from mediocrity, commercialism and/or untrue messages.

Amidst the sea of noise and litter, brands keep looking for loyal consumers with whom they can establish a fruitful dialogue. They are also searching for those famous Blue Oceans, free of attacks from the competition, an increasingly impossible mission.

Big brands generate completely out of control content by his followers and detractors, and there is no Community Manager in the world capable of handling these spontaneous demonstrations and harness them in the interest of the brands. The wave always passes them by and the only thing to do is let go, no spending splurge in digital communications, just keeping a testimonial presence for modernity's sake.

As far as the small brands, there is still a chance to act, but we must tread lightly to be noticed in the middle of the noise and litter. A real workforce of communication professionals must do this. True professionals, and there are very few of them.

Blue Oceans

Interview for the blog of Argentinean designer Norberto Baruch

1. In Buenos Aires, the latest online strategy has to do with the Blue Ocean theory. How can you reach out to non-customers if the potential of social media is not recognized?
I think Blue Ocean is a new way of calling niche-market positioning. In other words, find a place where your product is unique and therefore free from the threats of fierce competition from the traditional markets.

Of course, social networks can play a decisive role to find this Blue Ocean for our product.

2. It is argued that the Blue Ocean theory is an upgrade of Da Vinci's basic creative principles. What place does the creative act have in marketing today?
Creativity is and has always been the basis of all differentiation processes in the marketing world. Without creativity there is no possibility whatsoever for the Blue Oceans, new market niches and effective communication with consumers.
The new, original and unusual, is always outside the realm of logic and it manifests only in the land of creativity.

3. Why, according to Advertising Age Magazine, are marketing database companies being recognized as mega advertising agencies in the United States?
Today the individual has been relocated as the center of all strategies in this extraordinary expansion of social networks. The CRM is more important than ever, and these expert companies manage databases as a powerful communication tools from person to person.

4. Should Facebook, Twitter and MySpace users really know how their data is used?
I'm an advocate of full transparency; there should laws be a law in place to force all networks to communicate clearly and not in fine print the actual use of the data collected.

5. The algorithms used in marketing are to analyze data and classify consumers. Is it ethical this discriminatory exercise? It is not good to be considered a "waste".
To answer the previous question, if there is no transparency in the use of data, there are no acceptable ethics to qualifying us.

6. Does it help creating a Facebook fan community to get the much needed customer loyalty?
I think those are two things that have nothing to do with each other. You can be a fan of a brand on Facebook and not pursue it in any other platform. Statistics are numbers but loyalty has a much deeper link between the brand and the customers.

7. Which side would you take in the War of the F's? Foursquare or Facebook, why?
The level of popularity is still light years in favor of Facebook. I do not think that comparisons can be made today.

8. If anything characterizes Advertising 3.0 is its almost interpersonal arrival, one to one. But this approach is not always respectful. How can companies begin to respect the consumer?
I think that the consumer is increasingly the master of all processes of Internet 3.0, so the manipulation done by companies will be on the decline. The consumer is king and he or she decides how and when is his or her relationship with brands.

The new communication (1)

Advertainment and Advergaming.

For many years I have heard many advertisers claim the use of innovative media in all agencies. "Is there anything beyond television, radio, newspapers, magazines and outdoor advertising?" And the agencies are always reluctant to change using the excuse of the GRP to justify their inaction.

But in recent years, even the most recalcitrant is being forced to recognize that the status quo of the conventional media it's been scattered into pieces. Nobody can present a serious communication strategy without considering, not only the Internet or mobile phones, but also other less known techniques such as Advertainment or Advergaming, two branches of the same concept.

The common denominator of these two new ways to tackle advertising communication is to mix, or rather, melt advertising with entertainment and the message within the contents of the media, every advertiser's dream. Making your advertising an inseparable part of the content without interrupting the enjoyment of the client will engage and increase the realism to the proposed entertainment.

In the "Mission Zero" spot the viewer watches Uma Thurman drive in the streets of Los Angeles behind the wheel of a new Lamborghini Gallardo with Pirelli tires fleeing from fearsome murderers. This short piece is sponsored by the brand of tires and can only be seen on the Pirelli website where the viewer has an active role in the process, he or she is immersed in the message in a deliberate and natural way, choosing to be shocked and enjoy it.

Advertainment is here to stay and Rodrigo Figueroa Reyes and David Drogba perfectly and brilliantly understood the creative aspect, several years ago they created agencies specializing in this discipline.

As to Advergaming, the practice of using video games to fuse them with the advertising message is a growing phenomenon. There is virtually one game console in every US home and Europe will soon follow. That huge gamer potential has made close to 1,000 million dollars of advertising, a figure dramatically on the rise.

And a very important fact: until very recently the producers of video games would pay a significant amount of royalties to use their brand logos. However, Pizza Hat now pays Sega to have their Crazy Taxi game stop in one of their establishment. Play station receives money from Nike and Coca Cola to include their products in their virtual city streets.

Advertainment, Advergaming, Artvertising, Tryvertising ... and many other new forms of advertising are INROADS to the market. Breaking old patterns, outdated routines of the mainstream media, and opening a new panorama, fuelled with suggestive perspectives.

The new communication (2)

Trysumers and Tryvertising

Since the beginning of trade, brands would offered to their future consumers samples of their products; small portions of food in supermarkets and samples of cosmetics in the pages of women's magazines, also car dealers let us test drive their product. It is a known and common practice; in English it is called "trial".

But today, when communication is immersed in a frantic search for new ways and new roads outside the mainstream media, a powerful stream of new product testing comes into the playing field.
An overwhelming power that goes far beyond the usual concepts and baptized with a new name, "Tryvertising", not only in practice but they also have a name for their recipients, "Trysumers" a new generation of "testers", born, like almost everything today, under the Internet umbrella.

Since you have the possibility to purchase online second hand musical instruments, like electric guitars in auction sites such as EBay, and at very low prices, many young people who did not dare to buy a new guitar for fear of spending too much money, to then quit and leave the guitar lying on a corner, purchase cheap instruments. This gave them the opportunity to experience, at a low price, his or her musical vocation;

they then can be sure that if they buy a new and valuable instrument, without wasting their money.

Companies like Sony have taken product testing to a new and unexpected level giving all visitors to the New York Zoo the latest model of their video camera to use it during their visit, and when returned they received a disk with the recorded images to take home.
Nike customers test their shoes in different athletic events in the "Nike Trial Vans", stocked with 1,000 pairs of shoes of all sizes. Apple also allows customers to test their computers in their more than 170 stores.

All these actions will satisfy the needs of a new consumer profile that prefers to try everything before buying it and are immune to other types of advertising. The effect is similar to the experience most people feel before a delicious and varied buffet where the dishes are on display to awaken our appetite. The opportunity to try them allows us to make a satisfactory choice.

Three revolutions that "changed" the rules of advertising.

It is not new that the advertising industry is a mess and it seems that this will last many years to come. Too many events are taking place without pause and this prevents the sector to recover from the knock out. Imagine a referee's count goes to eight, them a new punch comes along.

Loss of influence with advertisers, drastic reductions in profitability, junior staff growth, separation between the media and the creative and disorientation about the future... are some of the evils plaguing advertising in recent years. But above all these circumstances, there are three great revolutions that dramatically changed the game.

The first revolution was the transformation of products into brands. This transition aimed at a society eager to consume products as a result of the industrial society and economic development, it started in the early twentieth century to a developed and saturated society where the products are no longer staples and became low added-value commodities.

In my conferences I explained many times that in the 50s and 60s products had differences between them and advertisers would rationally highlight those differences, so that the consumer would make an informed choice between them. The manufacturers did not think about the consumer, because the consumer would buy everything they produced. His obsession was to manufacture with the highest quality at the lowest cost, confident that their products would sell.

Later, in the 70s and 80s, emotion entered into the advertising proposals. More and more products offered the same features with the same level of quality, so it was necessary to add excitement to the message in order to differentiate one product from another. The concept of Marketing mix appeared, where the consumer is at the beginning and at the end of the whole process. It is no longer enough to make a product, now we have to make the product that the consumer demands.

The commercialization process must start and end in the consumer, so the value of the brand gains momentum. Today's products are not what they seem and their technological differences have an ephemeral nature because any competitor can copy any product almost immediately. It is necessary to have a strong brand above and beyond the product. A brand that will sell any product with its name, a brand associated with certain values fitted like a glove to the values demanded by the final user.

This conversion of products into brands gave rise to the second revolution of the advertising media industry: the revolution of contents. In a few years the advertising contents goes from a mere report on the advantages of the products, to the use of seduction as a weapon to attract consumers to later find empathy with the emotional relationship between these and the brands.

The brand was traditionally hidden inside the clothing but now it is shamelessly exhibited in all kinds of garments. The consumer flaunts his or her preferences to an extreme, like tattooing the Nike logo.

Times have changed and conventional advertising is no longer useful for the new consumer and o make matters worse, in came the third revolution; screens. Screens came to complicate everything. First the big screen (cinema) then television, after the computer and finally hard screens, iPods and mobile phones.

This creates a saturation of advertising messages and a growing disinterest in the part of the consumer. Advertising of the 90s, which was more interesting than the contents shown on the television, is now boring to the spectator, now they have to endure ads exceeding twenty minutes in length on all channels. Advertising interrupting the content is no longer frowned upon by anyone, and there is a growing demand for a much less aggressive advertising.

With this background, agencies are lost and submerged in a sea of confusion, overwhelmed by all these changes and for the moment unable to give an adequate response to their customers. Full service agencies, a strategic partner of high value to advertisers started dying when they concentrated solely on television, and now they are desperately trying to recover everything that was neglected.

They talk about new concepts such as integrated communication, a "360 degree" agency, these are communication companies rather than advertising agencies, but they still have not solved the modus operandi. A new generation of creative people truly integrated in new technologies and strategists specialized in branding development, and capable managers to understand the changes that have occurred in the sector will need to come to recover what has been lost.

And it better be quick because there are many new players, like large strategic consulting companies that are positioning themselves strongly in the market. Creativity and strategy are the most powerful weapons to build a brand image, the agencies know this, but sometimes they can no longer see the forest for the trees. Therefore, it is necessary to examine very thoroughly the changes that have occurred in recent years, the three great revolutions that have changed the industry and act accordingly, concentrating all our efforts on building a new agency model capable of providing solutions to the advertisers and consumers of today.

Do you also want to be creative?

It is quite common among advertising students to pursue his or her interests in creativity. It is very logical, because creativity is the axis on which the advertising industry pivots and creative people are the shining stars of the agencies.

However, although I am convinced that creativity is an attitude, a different way to tackle the everyday and therefore capable of being learned with training, not everyone is fitted to be a creative in advertising. Let me explain.

Curiosity, excitement, openness, flexibility, risk and imagination are the real keys to creative thinking. And it is necessary for a person who thinks in engaging in a creative practice to somehow have printed those key elements in his hard drive. He must also be open to all hypotheses and unusual learning ability.

Moreover, since advertising is a commercial bond established between consumers and brands, you must be fully trained in that department, something you have previously learned in college or other specialized centers before joining the scope of the agencies.

It is not enough to be creative; we must also learn the trade and understand the value of a commercial strategy and the role of creativity in the process of any marketing company.

Although the birth and development of ideas occurs following the same patterns for musicians, poets, painters, scientists and advertisers to develop campaigns, an added expertise is required. Copywriters and Art Directors are some of the specific positions for a creative in an advertising agency, and creativity is a skill required in each of their areas.
A Copywriter should be familiar with the language and its grammar; he must have confidence to move from specific word to abstract concepts and the Art Director must have training in graphics, design criterion and a special sensitivity to fonts, colors and spaces. If someone who wants to be a creative in advertising her or she must meet these conditions and then he or she can be ready to start his new career.

All agencies of the world are eager to hire talent. That is the secret of their business, the ingredient that gives them success. So when there is an awareness of not letting quality walk out of the door, a door open to an exciting profession like no other, filled with rewarding experiences.

A foreword of the book "Engagement Marketing"

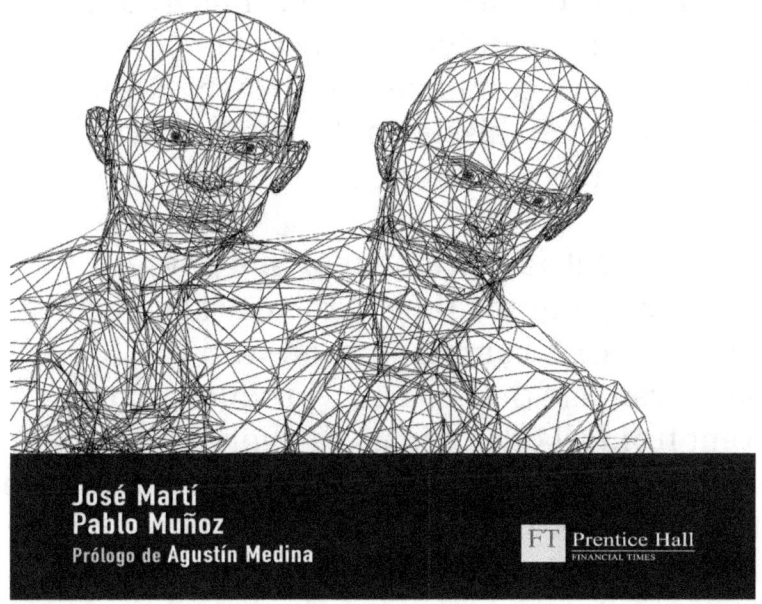

In the process of the Marketing Mix, which is to investigate consumer needs in order to produce later products to suit him, to then be forward to them through different distribution channels, a multitude of new factors compels us to review the entire process.

Since Rosser Reeves, CEO of the American agency and Ted Bates in the 50s, developed their famous creative philosophy USP (Unique Selling Proposition), proposing the differential advantage of the product as a unique selling point, some important things have happened in the world of advertising. First, the transformation of products into brands, a revolution in consumer choice affecting transcendental relations between the company and its clients. A change that has a lot to do with the advancement of technology and has virtually eliminated the differences between competitive products, completely destroying Rosser Reeves theses based precisely on the competitive differences of products and services.

Today, technological advancement or any physical difference has very limited time in the market, making it impossible to base a communication with the differential advantage that turned a product unique and different from all others in its category. The product was no longer attractive per se, and had to take refuge in the value of the brands that protect it. Today, consumers buy brands rather than products and this has revolutionized the contents of advertising communication. From the famous Marlboro Friday, on April 2, 1993, that became known as the day that brands died, the truth is that brands began to be more alive than ever.

Many companies decided to invest in promotion rather than in image, looking for short-term profits instead of a powerful and enduring brand. At that time, global investment in communication was at 70% in conventional advertising and 30% in promotional. Ten years later, the current situation is reversed, with 70% for promotional and only 30% for brand image. However, other brands like Starbucks, Nike, Apple, The Body Shop or Calvin Klein, decided to bet heavily on keeping their prices and investments on the image. They believed in the brand and eventually showed the world their success and the future belonged to them. Today, almost no one disputes that a brand is a thousand times more important than the products it represents. And if you have a good brand, you can sell any product.

The second revolution was content related. The products and their differences required to develop for the consumer an informative advertising showing all the differential advantages of the product. The product was the hero of a communication that was generally based on the typical pattern "problem-product-solution". But in the 70s and 80s, with the unstoppable rise of television, the demand for advertising competed with the contents of the media who then forced the advertisers to seduce their recipients. Pure and simple information led to the seduction, and it was so successful that viewers said that the ads were the most attractive aspect of television programming.

Later in the 90s, when the consumer stopped being astonished by the spectacle of ads, it was necessary to developing advertising that connected emotionally with the consumers; it established a stream of empathy between them and the brands, they no longer cared about the benefits of the product, now it was the brand that established a strong relationship with their customers. And if this was achieved, they were ready to buy whatever brand offered to them. The commitment becomes so strong that brand users have no problem displaying them in their own body. Chanel, Dolce & Gabbana and Armani stamp their logos on clothes proudly worn by their customers. And some of them, as in the case of Nike, have tattooed the famous symbol on their skin. According to her book "No Logo", Naomi Klein tells us that most Nike employees in the United States have a Nike tattoo, and in American tattoo parlors, the Nike logo has more demand than dolphins or black roses.

The third element that has revolutionized marketing communications has to do more with the evolution of image technologies. Certainly the visual element is dominant in relationships between customers and brands, so ever since the late nineteenth century, when the first modern advertising brands like Coca Cola or Vin Mariani decorated their ad text with attractive and evocative illustrations. Year's later, cinema and television would be the supporting protagonists of the brightest media advertising strategies. And today the computer, mobile phone and video game consoles have joined this festival of screens; along with plasma screens flooding cities like Tokyo, by offer the sender and the receiver of the communication a new universe of infinite possibilities.

We must add to this the interactive communication possibilities offered by Internet 2.0 and 3.0, an explosion some people have predict will happen by 2015. A network that will no longer be "virtual", it will come closer to a "reality" shared by microprocessors, sensors and applications that will interact with the concrete and material things. In the middle of it all is the "Engagement Marketing", a new model that represents a commitment with consumers, a farewell to the old days where publicity "interrupted" leisure time of the consumer to deliver the message. Now it is the consumer who chooses how, when and where in an exercise of freedom never seen before in our history.

The classic marketing techniques is surpassed by the transformation of products into brands.

Interview about my book "Bye, bye, Marketing"

Is marketing in crisis? Judging by the title of the book, it would seem dead.
- There is no doubt in my mind that marketing is in crisis, like almost all commercial and communication tools. And you can say that the old marketing of the twentieth century based on the famous 4Ps (Product,

Price, Place, Promotion) is now history. Now new business strategies cannot lose sight of the fifth P, People, the hub of all processes.

If marketing is dead, what or who killed him?
- He died a natural death. It was almost centennial and they were already weighing the ailments. In addition, everyone is determined to distort it, giving it a surname and new responsibilities. Mobile Marketing, Email Marketing, Buzz Marketing, Street Marketing, Field Marketing, Geo Marketing, Engagement Marketing ... and dozens more surnames, its too confusing. No doubt that marketing is not what it once was.

Throughout history, did advertising agencies created marketing to their customers? Has this situation changed?
In fact, marketing was invented by advertising agencies before professor Neil Borden from the Harvard Business School gave it a name in 1950. Marion Harper Jr. president of McCann-Erickson ordered the marketing tools that were used in isolation by companies like Coca Cola and Procter & Gamble since the late nineteenth century, and created the Full Service Agency that for many years was the marketing station of most companies.

Later, other companies created their own marketing departments, and along with the rise of television in the eighties, ended with the Full Service Agencies.

Is Internet also having something to do with all these changes?
Of course, and not just Internet. The classic marketing techniques have been overwhelmed by the transformation of products into brands, surge of the Internet and the rapid development of new technologies, the rise of mobile communications and the decline of the television are part of the transformation suffered by the media, and particularly with the abandonment of the passive attitude of consumers.

"From the power of the market to consumer power" is the subtitle of your book. Internally, the consumer was called "the boss". But many people think that the consumer is easily manipulated, often deceived. What is the truth of it?
- The consumer has never been manipulated. Even in the fifties, when the strong market demands didn't count on him for any business strategies. People know very well what they wanted and needed and all the manufacturers, brands, products and distributors could and can do is to be as close as possible to their demands.

Is there marketing behind private brands?
- I believe that private brands do not exist. All brands have connotations and values that make them unique. I do not think that El Corte Ingles Brand has the same value as Mercadona or the Día private Brand. It is certain that people distinguish very well the perceived quality of the ones and the others.

Finally, could you tell us who and why people should read your book?
I think "Bye, bye, marketing" is of great interest to all those who have made of marketing and communication their professions, but it is also for people who have some responsibility in the future of their companies. Because this book is aimed at understanding what is happening already into the future, an essential aspect for anyone looking to evolve in his or her profession.

The day the brands died

The low cost pioneers, direct heirs of private brands, invaded the tobacco sector in the United States in the early nineties. New brands of cheap cigarettes flooded point of sales and threatened the market shares of traditional brands like Philips Morris, with their the leading brand Marlborough, and they were was getting nervous. Their flagship was being mercilessly torpedoed in full view; a less intruder brand waving the flag of low prize adversely affected Marlboro sales. It was not yet a dramatic situation, only a few tenths of a point of lost shares, but the company executives trembled at the prospect of what was only the first sign of the catastrophe. Never before had anything like that happened and no one knew how far it could go.

They had no advertising costs, were not interested in creating a Brand or a long-term image, that allowed them to lower the price without damaging their image and maintaining their profit margins. In addition, a product like tobacco, where the consumer cannot perceive a clear difference between competitors, a price cut could be deadly. When tenths of a point became a full point drop in the percentage share of the Marlboro market, the men of Philips Morris could no longer resist, they had to compete with the same weapons as their opponents. If the game were to cut prices, they would do it risking a part of their profit margin to maintain sales volumes intact they lowered the price of Marlboro no less than 20%, an irresistible offer to consumers and for newcomers alike.

What the executives did not anticipate was the effect lower prices would have on the value of Philips Morris in the New York Stock Exchange, moved like all others, by blows of intuition, rumors and extreme sensitivities to the slightest change in the market. In this case, New York brokers realized that a brand as strong as Marlboro, that for 40 years had invested hundreds of millions of dollars in advertising campaigns with his famous cowboy, building a theoretical solid image to face any eventuality could be vulnerable, and this could only mean that the brand was useless. Therefore, the brand was dead and major brand companies didn't have anywhere near the value attributed to them.

Friday April 2, 1993 would go down in history as Black Friday of the New York stock exchange under the name of Marlboro Friday, the day that brands died. That day not only the prices of Philips Morris collapsed together with prominent companies known for their brands, such as Coca Cola, Pepsi Cola, Procter & Gamble, Nabisco or Heinz among others. Many marketing managers interpreted the crash as a sign to withdraw their image oriented advertising campaigns and reinforce all promotional activities at achieving short-term benefits.

And from that time on, many business schools began to train new generations of entrepreneurs in the philosophy of cutting expenses on image communication and short-term profitability. It is no coincidence that the proportion of the total investment between the higher and lower the line, which in 1993 was 70% and 30% respectively, in just 10 years was completely reversed.

However, some companies that started to develop in those years did not want to get into catastrophic dynamics and continued to invest heavily in the brand. Brands like Apple, Nike, The Body Shop, Starbucks or Calvin Klein decided to ignore the naysayers and gradually showed that they were right and that the future belonged to them. Even Philips Morris, after the first moments of bewilderment, backtracked their steps and raised the prices for Marlboro.

In 1995, two years after the fateful Marlboro Friday, the brand had not only recovered their share participation, but they were also increased by 9%, from 22% to 31%, thus demonstrating that their brand, built by many years of money in advertising, was able to resist the hardest blows of price competitiveness.

Brand and the brand image

The image of things is always more important than the things themselves, together with our context of brands and products, the former being the image of things and the products the latter. Today there is no doubt about the importance of the ones and the others. In the first paragraph of his magnificent book "No Logo" Naomi Klein makes this clear: "It is legitimate to say that the astronomical growth of wealth and cultural influence of multinational companies, occurred over the past 15 years, stems from a unique and apparently harmless idea, that successful companies must foremost produce brands and not products".

Brands are powerful because they are pure image and the image is pretty much the only thing that counts in all areas of our lives. We fall in love with actresses or actors for the roles they play but were horrified to discover that Rock Hudson, the symbol of masculinity in the 60s and 70s, was homosexual, or that the sparkling and sexy Marilyn Monroe was a very unhappy woman. Everyone agrees that Picasso was a genius, but most people do not understand or like his painting. And we are convinced that all Scottish people are stingy, the Japanese are disciplined and the Germans are square heads; because that's the image we have created of them.

Almost always we rely more on images than in reality itself but if we take a closer look, the rationale behind this power of the image is in the need our memory has to keep as little as possible detailed information for each recall, but we only need a few elements to compose the entire memory. *According to a study of an English University, it is not important the order in which the letters are written. The only important thing is that the first and the last letter of every word are in the correct position.* This means that when we see a car with BMW or a Mercedes brand, for example, we do not need to know in detail its technical characteristics to assume that this is a quality car, attributed entirely to the positive image we have of said brands. Nor we need additional data than the brief acronyms to know that MNG means Mango, D&G Dolce and Gabbana and CKNY Calvin Klein New York. Also, we identify by a single stroke the Nike brand and immediately recognize the best values of sportsmanship.

The way we perceive images is very important because the image is the essence of a brand, or in other words, the only major business in reality. An American industrialist left behind in writing, in the early twentieth century, the following: *"If I had to choose between losing my factories or lose the reputation of my products, gained by advertising for the past twenty years, I will not hesitate, I would destroy the factories, you can build new factories in three months, but there is no capital capable of doing the same with the image of my products, nor capable of recovering twenty years of good advertising".*

Today those words are truer than ever. Undoubtedly the greatest asset of a company is its brand. A company is no more than an abstract entity embodied by the products they produce or the services they provide. And these in turn, are specified in the brands they represent; so the intangible heritage of businesses is actually the only truly tangible one.

How to build a brand

Today nobody denies the importance of having a good brand but, as I have commented in previous articles, however, people still don't have it clear the differences between the image of the brand name and the products it shelters.

David Ogilvy wrote that there is always a product behind the brand, but not always a brand behind a product. The brand is defined through a personality that makes it unique, just as it happens with humans that for some reason stand out above all others, whose characteristics that make them unique and admired are the variables constituting his personality. Not all great athletes have one, or all actors, even politicians who were once the most voted.

Personality is worth millions to few people, and only those who have it remain in the memory forever. The first key of personality for a brand is knowledge, which is the sum of a spontaneous and suggested notoriety. Without knowledge there is no brand, but knowledge is not in itself sufficient to create it.

The second important key is Perceived Quality, which is very different to quality per se, since an emotional approach only has value when the recipient receives the quality of the brand, independent of her tangible reality.

The brand identity emerges through the attributes that her target audience perceives, and is a basic element to define her personality. The attributes should be clear, well defined and can be of a rational nature based on the physical characteristics of the brand, or of an emotional nature, which are often the most important because they are the ones that are recorded strongly in the depths of the feelings of any consumer, and make it a part of their lives.

Finally we have Fidelity, the real yardstick for measuring customer satisfaction. They say it costs five times more to get a new customer than to keep an old one. Therefore it is very important for the brand to create this cozy feeling that makes it familiar and indispensable.

Few brands meet all these requirements and if value were tested on these four parameters as for big brands, like Coca Cola for example, we see quite clearly that this is really a brand that stands out with flying colors on Knowledge, Perceived Quality, Identity and Fidelity.

If your brand can also withstand this test, congratulations are in order, but if don't, do not waste you're time and start using wisely all the tools to build a good brand.

Of course, you can continue to rely on traditional media, but you cannot just settle on them because they have become more and more expensive and even more saturated. Take television for example; according to the prestigious firm Forrester Research, 76% of advertising executives in the United States believe that the traditional 30" TV spot will be dead in 10 years. There are already brands like the Australian Foster's Lager Beer who gave up on television to appeal to their younger customers through the Internet, using the slogan "Because TV sucks."

The media where the message constantly interrupted content is no longer fashionable. The interruption marketing has given way to engagement marketing and now consumers prefer Advertainment, a place where advertising intelligently merges with the content. The proper use of conventional media and new media are good tools for building brands.

Do as you like, but get a brand with strong a personality and only then you will be able to sell your products. As my admired Naomi Klein says: "Companies can engage in manufacturing products, but consumers are only interested in buying brands".

A name is not a brand

Many people swimming in the field of Marketing and Communications confuse the name with the brand and think that finding a good name for their products is more than enough, like a short and simple name, easy to remember and that could define the use of the product and the attributes of the image they want the product to portray. However, the name of a product usually has nothing to do with its success, although I know this statement may awaken the cholera of companies that earn fortunes by designing name strategies and charging desperate and incredible figures.

As far as names are concerned, there is no logic in the world of brands.
Sometimes they are a product of chance, and the initial logic with which it was created becomes disrupted when crossing the border of language. I made it very clear fifteen years ago in a seminar of the Instituto de Empresa when I spoke about the power of brands, and gave hundreds of examples to illustrate how wide and capricious this particular subject can be.
Brands like Lois, initially intended to sound like a foreigner translated the name of a company director into French. The manager was called Luis, but the translator wasn't so good and neglected to use the "u" in the translation, and instead of Louis (French for Luis), ended up calling it Lois (Law in French). In any

73

case, without Luis and with Law, Lois ended up being a success in the French, Spanish and many other markets.

There are other brands that meet all orthodoxy in their language of origin such as Close Up or Mr. Proper, but outside Anglo-Saxon countries, they mean nothing to people who do not understand English. And such is the case that, depending on market circumstances, one of those brands had to be renamed from Mr. Proper to Don Limpio (Mr. Clean), without any fuzz, and consumers continue buying the product anyway.

Unpronounceable brands for most Spaniards like Schweppes have flourished in our country, and others like Mercedes -they themselves have said that the name came from of the wife or daughter of the founder of the company- a symbol of luxury and elegance worldwide. Could you imagine an airline or a computer company called Mary Lou? It would not be any different than Apple, that for Americans is also a simple apple, with the added stress that its flagship Macintosh was named after a variety of apples, as if we were to cal it Manzana Reineta here in Spain. Very few would dare to put this name on an international leader company in the world of computers. Even more, the Apple logo is a drawing of a bitten apple.

The brands are not born, but made, just like people, we develop a personality on our lifetime and through our actions and in the end the name you have doesn't really matter. All that matters is what we build behind that name. It doesn't matter if it is a short and simple name like Messi, Torres or Nadal, or a long and complicated as Severiano Ballesteros. Millions of people around the world know who they are, although most of them do not know how pronounce their names properly.

Is anyone really an expert in social networks?

There are hundreds of comments every day in all media outlets about the effectiveness of social networks. And most of these comments are contradictory, to say the least.

"Social networks are the only future of communication". "Social networks have had their days". "Social networks service communities of interest, but they do not sell a product or develop a brand". If you're not on any social network you do not exist". "50% of all U.S. companies are not on any social network". "Advertising on a social network is very cheap". "Advertisement on social networks is very expensive relative to its questionable effectiveness". Etc.

The only indisputable fact is that everyone wants to be in social networks because today is the most-advanced vehicle to communicate with the rest of the world. Even companies think that if they are not present they are missing something out and it can hit the fan in the future.

There are some curious hard facts; there are about 1,000 million Facebook users in the world, one in six of the population of our planet, YouTube gets about 4,000 million daily visits, and there are 500 million Twitter users and 200,000 Linkedin members. And the numbers grow steadily; it's an unstoppable force.

I recently read somewhere that as far as social networking, nobody knows anything for sure, and there are no professors or doctors in this field. We are all just students.

I think that's a very true statement.

MAD MEN

In December 15, 1960 I was fourteen and two days earlier I started working as an errand boy in the largest advertising agency in Spain called Ruescas. It had 120 employees and had most American brands that in those years returned to the Spanish market. Winston and Camel cigarettes, Champion spark plugs, Palmolive soap and Colgate toothpaste were some of our major customers. Three years later, in 1963, McCann Ericson landed in Spain and bought one hundred percent of the shares of Ruescas. The agency was renamed Ruescas-McCann Ericsson and all working methods were immediately adapted to the standard of Madison Avenue. We all learned to be Mad Men.

The more I see the TV series, the more I admire the writers for the fine work they've created, an accurate depiction of what the advertising agencies were in the sixties. An exciting and glamorous atmosphere filled with brilliant minds flowing in alcohol, cigarettes, sex and ambition, with the added challenge of understanding the new invention that was changing everything i.e. television.

The Mad Men of the sixties were filled with enthusiasm to conquer television. They were seasoned in print media advertisement, great copywriters and art directors who forged their careers in the pages of newspapers and magazines. They also handled with great proficiency the radio, the media king in the 40a and 50a. But the whole experience was little or no help applying it to the media that was winning in the audience in rankings. So much so that in Ruescas, McCann-TV was the exclusive responsibility of an Australian named Frank Boss, he was the only creative specialist in that field, and no one else in the agency was involved in television commercials. He was the sole responsible for writing the scripts, choosing the production companies and supervising the whole process. It can be said that the big announcements the agency produced in the mid sixties were exclusively his work.

Naturally, given the importance of television and its unstoppable growth of customers, all creative agencies were incorporated in the process of preparing advertisements. I did it in 1965, when I started to develop as copywriter and assistant to Charlie Burlakow, the creative director of the agency. So you can say that my career as a creative has a special link to television, as it was for all of my generation, we were taking our first steps together with the new medium itself.

Our generation achieved success as television creative in the golden decade of the eighties, where Spain shared awards and international recognition with England and the USA, certainly the masters of the genre. What I foresaw in 1980, the first time I went to the Cannes Festival as a jury was that "Spain would be the third creative power of the decade" In those days, the

English magazine Campaign asked me for an article about Spanish creativity and I dared to write my quoted above. The English men were so amazed that they highlighted the sentence on the cover of the magazine. They, as well as all the other countries, could attest to it some years later.

Television has not died yet as it was preached by some, but most certainly it's not what it was. TV spots are increasingly boring and disruptive of our leisure time with insufferable and really obnoxious segments. Moreover, because of the emergence of the Internet, the users of this new media have discovered the power of choice and this is revolutionizing everything. The consumer does not want to be constantly interrupted by advertising and demands his more direct involvement with the content. And will only be willing to endure it, if that union is entirely satisfactory for him.

Moreover, the routine of the conventional media of the twentieth century has been broken into pieces. Creativity is flooding the streets with new formats; there are digital media sweeps on all screens, transgressing the old boundaries of television and cinema, operating on computers, mobiles, consoles or plasma screens. Mad Men must face again a prodigious decade from their particular working environment, definitely very different to those happy sixties, where the old advertising is no longer valid for the future. New times require new solutions and those who are starting have the enormous task ahead. They must forget the brilliance of the old Mad Men, but their example should help them face the new task with enthusiasm and the assurance that they will also shine in the new media, like their predecessors with television, where history found a place for them as media icons and to star on a TV series 50 years after.

The Devalued Lions of Cannes.

I have been part of the jury at the Cannes Film Festival twice. The first time was back in 1980, I was merely a boy when the year the prodigious decade of advertising was worldwide phenomena, a year that started the shift from rational to emotional in advertising, where creativity triumphed over any other parameters of judgment, and the last year where the jury was composed only by the creative. The organization did not like our statement that the Grand Prix was as dry as a desert, and our objections to the excessive amount of gold medals awarded in each of the categories. So they made sure that creative madmen never be part of the jury.

The public did not like our view and the day of the awards we had to leave the Festival Palace escorted by French police, the public threw at us everything at the ceremony, from toilet paper to the most varied products of French horticulture. Everyone in Cannes loves to get prizes, and if they do not get one they can become very angry. In fact, agencies worldwide vowed never to return to the festival, but a year after, their enrollment doubled. And the golden years that followed showed that we were the reason for them being so stingy with the awards.

The Lions then became a very serious award, if you got one you were at the top of our business and that's why they were so important for creative and advertising agencies.

In 2002, when I was invited to be part of the jury for the second time, the Lions remained the highest award you could receive in advertising. But after, not so long ago, television remained the king of media together with their top rated Lions and Graphic Lions. Even the festivals started to develop into other categories such as Media, Direct Marketing and Interactive Advertising.

Today, with an agonizing television and the digital media growing at astronomical speeds, there are many categories in Cannes to win a Lion and thus having their income multiplied. But I fear that the power the Lion once had has been diminished at an inverse rate of their profits.

Today the Lions are distributed left and right to the delight of the organization and the winners. But I wonder if a Lion today has the same value as a Lion from before, I fear they have reached a level of complacency never seen before, and the advertising world seem sadder than ever. Cannes has seen better days, but it is now reinventing itself with fewer categories assuming the reality of our times, and drastically reducing the prized Lions. Could they roar again with the same power as before?

The basis of advertising

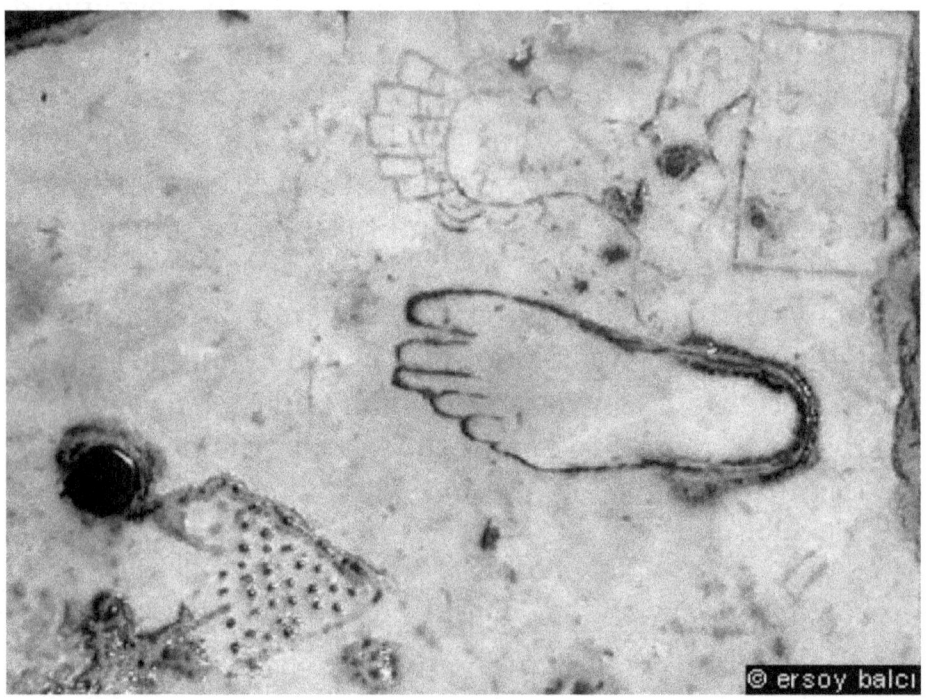

There is evidence that advertising is as old as the pyramids of Egypt, evidence found in papyrus, hieroglyphs etc. which shows irrefutable proof of product advertisement. It is only logical that from the first moment a person had something to sell, he or she had to advertise his product, whether orally, in paper or in stone. I had the opportunity to see an ad from 500 B.C. in the city of Ephesus, birthplace of one of my most admired philosophers for having formulated the following aphorism; "No man ever steps in the same river twice, for it's not the same river and he's not the same man."

Heraclitus

The ad reproduced in this post is a poster carved on a marble slab located in a corner of the main street of Ephesus. In it we see a foot indicating an address and also the head of a woman who, judging by the ornaments, it was apparently a prostitute.

We can easily guess that there was a brothel near by, clear and simple message with all the ingredients of any modern advertisement, such as; the "what", "how", the "to whom" and in this case also the "where".

What am I going to communicate? There is a brothel in that direction.

How am I going to communicate it? With a graphic form of advertising.

To whom was it intended? To all pedestrians of the city.

Where am I going to communicate my message? In the most central and traffic filled city street.

A clear, simple and probably very effective modern advertising strategy, a lesson in pragmatism to many current advertising agencies, that judging by the ads we see every day, have not yet understood the basic and elementary keys of communication, regardless of the means and technologies used.

Green ads on the highway

I confess I had never seen nor imagined floral advertising at the roadside. Beautifully sculpted commercial brand logos in hedges or on the grass adorning the side of an urban highway.

I saw them a couple of weeks ago in the city of Lima, and I could not believe it, in fact, it took me so long to react that I only had time to take a bad picture with my cell phone.

I could not get more than a piece of the logo of a bank, but I could see that the city was full of similar announcements. Magnificent hedges in the shape of letters and symbols of major companies in the middle of dense rush hour traffic.

Speaking of these urban "billboards" I remembered when the centers of our cities was full of 3 X 8 meters posters, and roadside billboards across the country were sprinkled with large format ads, it was then decided that they could pose a danger to drivers and a law was pronounced to eliminate all of them. Only the Osborne logo of the bull remains after a long debate, and was allowed to stay, it is also a symbol of Spain transcending its commercial significance.

I wonder if the Lima hedges distract the drivers and put them in danger or an oasis in the middle of the chaotic city traffic.

Moreover, it would be interesting to know how the City Council of Lima charges advertisers for the use of those spaces, or if there is a deal where the brands become responsible to provide maintenance, and under which conditions. No one could give me an answer, but everyone knows that the advertisers were in charge of maintenance.

When the Berlin Wall was decorated with graffiti.

In May 1990, just six months after the obsolescence of the wall, there were still several meters across the city intact. Including sections near the famous Brandenburg Gate, where we decided to shoot our Suzuki Vitara spot.

Luis Lopez de Ochoa and I travelled to Berlin with La Banda (our agency), and the brothers Agustin and Carlos Mejias were part of the Enigma Production Company. In the script, our car would cross the wall and triumphantly breaking the barrier between East and West in search of freedom, this shot required a long and unbroken piece of the wall.

We found wall bereft of graffiti because the East Germans chipped away layers of cement into small pieces to sell to tourists as souvenir.

Our production team recruited the help of local graffiti artists who painted again our piece of wall, but we could never imagine that at night, people came and chipped away our piece of the wall to sell as souvenir, this forced us to recruit more graffiti artists to reproduce our stolen graffiti trying to match our previous work with the help of the production still photography's, not to loose continuity.

This happened in each of the four days of shooting, so we ended painting a total of 800 meters that ended in thousands of fake-wall small pieces passing of as authentic. The piece you see here, I think is the real deal; I got it in a secluded area of the city, untouched by tourists and pickers.
Anyway, I cannot swear by a similar production of our film could have been done anywhere in Berlin that, at the time, was an explosion of joy, of freedom hungry East Berliners.

Rock and advertising

I had not heard about Mariskal in years, including our Christmas or less orthodox cards we exchanged each year he used to send me from different parts of the world, always with a crazy fun message befitting his overwhelming personality.

Suddenly, a few weeks ago, he send me an email inviting me to run a program on his www.mariskalrock.com station devoted to advertising. I was invited together with Rafael Balades and Manolo Valmorisco. I run into Manolo occasionally, the last time I was giving a conference at the University of Valladolid. I have not seen Rafael Balades for many years, but we have a common history dating back to when we were both about twenty something and filled with personal and professional dreams.

Rafael and Manolo are two major figures in advertising in Spain and each of them responsible of extraordinary campaigns that have made history. Rafael also is the author of "Freedom without anger", a song recorded in 1976 together with the launching of Diario 16, this song ended up being the anthem of the Spanish Transition.

The three of us shared, with Mariskal Romero unforgettable moments of our advertising vicissitudes. Mariskal is the king of Heavy Metal, not only in Spain but also in many parts of Latin America, especially in Argentina and Mexico. He has collaborated with the best DJs in the two major European music stations: Radio Luxembourg and BBC, and is the founder of the record label "Chapa" from Safiro records, bedrock of the great explosion of rock in Spanish, from the "movida" of Madrid in the 80's to the entire Latin American cultural market, producing bands like Obús, Leño, Mermelada, Asfalto, Bloque, Cucharada or Tequila among others. Currently he alternates his work between Spain and Argentina, producing radio concerts and editing the magazine "Heavy".

In advertising, and as far as I'm concerned, Mariskal and I collaborated on many rock-advertising campaigns, from a radio program for a Schweppes Tonic called "Leaving the basement," that helped launch young rock groups of the 80s, to recording of the soundtrack of the spot of the first Suzuki car sung by Mariskal himself. We also collaborated in campaigns for the young people's department of El Corte Inglés or Cimarron, these were the first spots of jeans filmed outside Spain, starting a trend that continued with other brands (Lois, Alton, Marlboro, Grin's, etc.) those were the brightest years of Spanish advertising.

The recording of the program on this last 29th was a great moment for all of us; we listened and talked about the great rock songs more closely related to our respective advertising experiences. Then we went together to eat and enjoyed some very affectionate hours remembering the old days.

Great and a long rock and roll life filled with glory to the ineffable Mariskal Romero.

1900 Russian advertising

I was convinced that the first advertising announcements using technique similar to the current one always came from the United States, the birth of Coca Cola in 1896, the starting point of modern advertising, the professionalism of the content and the elegance of the design could be considered high level.

However, on a recent visit to St. Petersburg I purchase a copy of a book of ads and Russian posters dating back to the last decade of the nineteenth century. I discovered that their quality was not only comparable to that of American ads, but in many cases the elegance and sophistication of the layout and the images was even better.

Advertisements of very different products such as alcoholic beverages, cigarettes, food, coffee, railways, postcards, entertainment, sewing machines, etc. all of them dated between 1890 and 1910, with an impressive advertising quality.

Since the 1917 revolution, advertising disappears to make way for the magnificent posters we all know, extolling the virtues of the Soviet Union with high quality designs, with the same quality as any like any country in the area of northern Europe. Nothing surprising thus far, but what is truly amazing is that there was a powerful advertising industry before the revolution, with spectacular quality.

Have you already tried the Google Glasses?

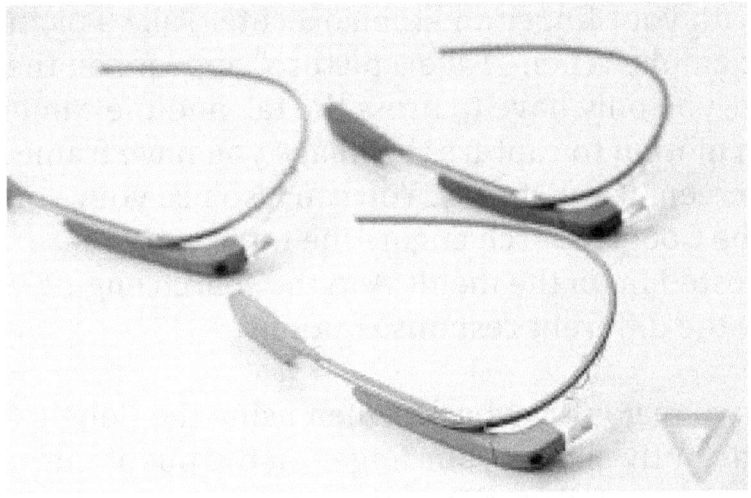

I could try them on last week during my participation in the II event of Innovation Talks, organized by IAB Spain.

The truth is that it was an interesting, exciting and disturbing experience. It is weird to see with the left eye the real perspective and with the right a small window that brings you into the digital world. It's a kind of ceremony of confusion; it definitely takes some practice to get used to. The real world and the infinite world of information and digital opportunities presented to you in two dimensions and your brain must learn to make them compatible.

On the small right eye screen you get a classic menu with different options you can select using the right pin of the glasses by moving a finger along the pin, toward your ear, so that the menu slides across the screen. When you find the item you're interested, you tap the pin with your finger and then execute. Take a picture, for example. When "Take a picture" appears on the menu, you only have to press the tab and the camera is set in motion to capture the image you have framed on the screen. It's that easy. You can also use your voice to tell the Google search engine the topic you are interested in on the menu. And the search engine will show the different response options.

The two major drawbacks when using the Google Glass is constantly sliding your finger on the pin of the glasses, or to talk to the system to request information. Imagine you are walk down the street talking to yourself and shaking your hand in front of your face. It sounds a bit like a human robot or a citizen of the universe in Orwell's 1984".

To solve these problems, a Spanish engineer has developed and patented a special remote control for Google Glass, a device that can easily be carried in the pocket, without having to be close to the glasses. His name is Juan Carlos Barambones and his company Remote Glass will undoubtedly be an objective to be followed by Google because, as they themselves have expressed, the Google Glass is still in process of improvement. Do not be surprised that the invention of the Spanish engineer could be incorporated in some way to the future development of the project.

Smartphone: Our sixth damned sense

Some days ago, my daughter and I were watching on the TV the terrible scenes where soldiers were shooting against the protesters causing hundreds of deaths and injuries in Egypt, then my daughter Barbara made me realize that many of the protesters, instead of worrying for their life, were recording the moment with their smart phones.

Ever since, I've been paying attention to this phenomenon in almost every television and newspaper, the number of people caught in the middle engaged in photographing or videotaping the scene is amazing. It seems to me that the recorded events through the lens of a mobile phone removed all relevance to the reality of whatever is happening, it is like as if the virtual world on the screen removes you from any reality at all, it's as if you were following it from your living room on a TV screen.

I shudder when I think that the mobile, which is already an appendix of our body, a sixth sense so to speak, with taste, touch, sight, hearing and smell, can also be an enemy of all our other senses placing them in a sort of a dormant state, isolated from reality and dropping our defenses, exposed to the bullets.

We already knew that the mobile phone isolated us and reduced the scope of our physical relationships, but never to the point of eliminating our sense of survival.

Anonymous beings

Until the late twentieth century, most of the inhabitants of this planet were anonymous beings, at best, a few hundred people had any news of our existence: close relatives, friends, co-workers and colleagues who share our same interests.

Fame was the privilege, or the opposite, of a few, whose activity was worthy of using up space in the mass media. However, fame has always been a secret desired by most humans. Andy Warhol already predicted that television would give many people the chance to have 15 minutes of fame, and he was right. For those 15 minutes some people are willing to give up their life and of course, they are willing to sell their privacy, honor, conscience, and even their soul if necessary. The success of all kinds of reality television shows, in the last twenty years, can attest to that. This display of intrusion is the most direct antecedent of the state of the current social networks.

Today, with social networking, we've emerged from obscurity to be the focus of attention, if you will, trapped in the vast media network displaying our ideas and our idiocy, show the world our skills and shamelessly displaying our daily lives through a carousel of inconsequential slides.

The great showcase of our vanity is the most successful aspect of the social networks. That is why they are so important and have a future, because of the promise of social reputation connected with the utopia of our own transcendence. A very interesting topic to follow, but because of its metaphysical significance it transcends the limits of this modest post in my blog.

Internet is a minefield

Like most Internet users, I receive hundreds of spam mail everyday, offering all types of ill-advised businesses like Viagra and other pharmaceutical products for penis enlargement, prevention of premature ejaculation, or improve in a hundred ways our sex life, they even offer sexual omnipotence. I do not know very well what it is all about, but sounds very exhausting. I also get job offers in which they promise me thousands of Euros without moving from home to represent Spain with world-renowned brands that could make me a millionaire in a few weeks. But if I put real estate for sale, very few interested people call me to set up a visit, but I get lots of overseas offers by email from buyers who want to close the deal immediately, just because they've seen the photos on Idealist.

I also receive letters of banks where I'd never had an account, proposals to get a College degree without ever attending any classroom. I have received threats to destroy a package with my name in it on an alleged courier if I do not answer immediately their requests for information. Lately, I have received marriage proposals from wonderful Russian women, same picture different names, but I guess that if I call Nadia, and/or Irina, I know that behind those angelic faces an artful Mafioso called Boris, Ivan and Vasili is hiding.

Deceptive Internet chats, where a 50-year-old pederast plays the part of a sweet 15-year-old teenager to steal

your privacy and/or money in the name of personal enjoyment, available to a network of undesirables like him. And the word "free", in ninety-nine percent of the deals, is a lying and deceiving vehicle rolling in the network. If you want to download an e-book, for example, they will tell you that it's free only if you register, but then they ask for a "symbolic" amount to maintain the operability of the system, and if you do not pay, there is no book or movie or football game or program for you to download.
All this is really awful and untactful, but I'm afraid that the Internet still has a worse side to it: false information circulating in millions of web pages. You can write, for example, that Christopher Columbus was an aeronautical engineer and a contemporary disciple of Leonardo Da Vinci, who was a famous chef and a close friend of Ferran Adria, and together they conducted the breakdown of the omelet in a night spree on Easter Island. Many people blindly believe it because they found on Google.
Anything found in the magical search engine is likely to become true and be repeated in thousands of blogs every day; this subculture expands across the five continents.

If it's not on the Internet it does not exist and the Network is already the new God for millions of individuals following the apostles reincarnated in the form of social networks. Meaningless postmodern culture of exchange with "Much ideology, but very few girls," as the Argentine rocker Moris wrote in one of his most famous songs of the late seventies. "A lot of verbiage, but few ideas," he wrote of today's Internet content. Verbiage also dishes out loads of garbage and misinformation.

Advertising in ruins

In the crisis of 2003 more than 700 advertising agencies were closed in Spain, but when the market rebounded in 2005, 500 new agencies were opened. Some of these new agencies currently occupy the top ranking of creativity and visibility within the sector. This is not a random event; it is simply the old axiom of the evolution of the species. When there is change there is evolution, but this depends solely on major changes, where everything is upside down we are forced to build everything again.

Weak and cheap creativity

It seems that we are in one of those critical moments when the foundations of the established order is threaten by ruin. Wherever you look the landscape seems bleak and confusing. Customers no longer trust agencies as they did before, they do not respect their strategic capability, knowledge of the media, intuition to open new roads or their capacity as marketing visionaries, they seem only to set up superfluous creativity dressed up with as decorative strategic objectives others have done before them. And obviously, they do not want to pay for what they do not do, nor are willing to pay too much for what they actually do.

Resistance to change

Meanwhile, the agencies seem content doing and receiving less and less and are incapable to really understand all the evils that, in the last ten years, have been growing in their backyard, the technological revolution that has the best players of yesteryear warming benches, and incapable of signing new contracts because they are not quite sure of the changes to be made. The fact is that they will lose the new game by a landslide because they may not understand the new rules. Specialists in new technologies do not always understand advertising theory and communication. Conventional agencies are bereft of marketing communication, because strategy and marketing have fled the agencies to take refuge in the winter quarters of advertisers. In addition, poor wages have put a stop to learning programs in the US together with internal quality training.

An opportunity for the braves

Fortunately, every dark moment of a crisis brings a new opportunity for the bravest. My advice is for you to have the courage to forget the past, to break with everything, to dig in the ruins and make a hole to establish new foundations, dare to build a new, brighter, more disruptive and the best current bid. The market is joyfully pleading to welcome advertisers to make their lives easier and to help them avoid the hassle of searching various potential partners to address the same problem. They enthusiastically welcome new strategic and creative means to move freely in the new media landscape unmetered from old concepts and repeated patterns.

Show them that you are different and charge handsomely for it, do not make the mistake of linking your quota with the Diasporas of the media. Your strategies and ideas are to be the backbone of your income and make sure you charge well for this because it is the best value per investment you can find in advertisement. And the survival of their brands depends on this very important foundation, which is, at the same time, the survival of their companies. It is time for a revolution to change everything and make people really notice that we are in the twenty-first century. It is now or never.

Boring creativity, outdated agencies

I think everyone connected with communication and marketing knows very well the changes that happened in the last twenty years in consumer advertising, the media and the brands.

I also assume that everyone is aware of the obsolescence of the advertising agencies from the twentieth century, old ads, old marketing strategies, old business structures, old working systems, the outdated client-agency relationships and obsolete rewarding and remuneration...

However, despite the general awareness of these topics, everything continues to be business as usual in the world of agencies, as if nothing had happened. Everyone is longing for better times, but resistance to change is stronger than his or her lamentations.

I fear that the large groups in control, WPP, Interpublic, Omnicom, Publicist, and Havas, etc. can care less where the benefits come from. They own everything that moves in communication, and if agencies are not doing well by outweighing the benefits of the media centers, it's because of their reluctance to dismantle their structures to create new ones. This entails too much work for a sector that has always been conservative in nature.

Then we have managers of agencies being hostage to the creative controlling power, they have the upper hand and do not want to become aware of the new times. They are old and one step away of early retirement, and don't like to get in trouble with Internet and social networks, which to them are like social climber brats. They still prefer the conventional thirty-second television spot, what people really see and what gives you fame and awards at festivals.

Everybody's house is dirty and the ads are becoming more boring and ineffective day by day.

Opportunity for entrepreneurs

It is not well seen to be an entrepreneur in Spain. The desire to undertake big enterprises usually gets confused with the desire to become rich at the expense of others. We are educated to be employed, and if possible, with a fixed and guaranteed working salary for life, one of our biggest handicaps when it comes to creating wealth and jobs.

In fact, only three in ten University graduates think of starting a business after school, compared to eight in every ten in the United States.
It is no coincidence that most of our entrepreneurs become one by accident, chance, or because it is his or her last resort. We must use the crisis to change this perception and show everyone that we have ideas and are very capable able to implement them. We can do miracles with our battered economy if we believe in ourselves and dare to rely a little more in ourselves.

I encourage all young people to see the future ahead as a virgin land; you have nothing to lose by trying and many years ahead to do it again and again if you fail the first time, I assure you that there is nothing more rewarding than seeing your idea and your business grow. Anyone who have walked this path before you, successful or not, will tell you that the experience was always worth the try.

Learning to follow through.

Foreword to the book "Mentoring for Entrepreneurs"

The economic fabric of a nation like Spain relies definitely on the quantity and quality of its SMEs. 99% of the companies can be considered in that definition. More specifically, 75% of them are small SMEs, despite the redundancy, and have only between one and five employees. It is vital, therefore, to develop a country where thousands of people every year undertake the adventure. And I stress adventure, because in these times of permanent crisis the undertaking has always been present.

Being an entrepreneur is a high-risk profession where you risk your money, your faith, your enthusiasm, your passion and your personal prestige, particularly in a country where entrepreneurs have never been too highly regarded. Schools and Universities have always taught us to be employed, or better yet, officials with a job and a safe salary. It is no coincidence that only three out of ten University students in Spain are ready to undertake any independent life after graduation, compared to eight in every ten students in the United States.

There are a number of entrepreneurial uncertainties and gaps in skills, sometimes because of lack of experience and sometimes because an excess of bad experiences of the older ones. The fact is that every entrepreneur faces their adventure from a different perspective, but the risks are common to all, because in practice, things are never as they were taught in the Universities. The development of ideas is a complex one, and you can never know if it was a good or bad idea until tested in the real world.

In my personal experience, it would have been useful to get good advice on all matters beyond my particular area of expertise. After many years of successful professional activity as advertising creative, I would have loved to learn management skills, financial, corporate issues, human resources, customer services or even real estate. I was never prepared for that, and had to learn everything from scratch with hard experiences and small failures, but I slowly learned the right way to develop my business.

When I wrote my book "Roadmap for Entrepreneurs", I wanted to help all new entrepreneurs to avoid the obstacles I had to face when creating a company. To take a hard look at what motivated you to become one, and re-evaluate your expectations, risks, independence, resources, partners, staff and the hard realities, and how to contribute to the corporate culture of which we are all so needy in the early stages.

Learning to undertake and prevent errors and taking advantage of the experience of others. That is the spirit of my book, and that is also the spirit of the mentors referred to in the book "Mentoring for Entrepreneurs Handbook" by Julio Rodríguez Díaz, a practical guide for mentors or mentees interested in adding value to their enterprise, by giving them professional experience and learn the vital skills for them to develop.

The book explains in detail the basic concepts of mentoring; the profile each of the participants must have, the processes to be followed during the relationship and all documents necessary to perform and develop. The book also includes testimonials, where the mutual relationship is of the utmost importance, a few examples:

"From the first meeting with my mentees I realized the benefits of the program. Giving advice has helped me reflect on management issues. I'm surprised at how rewarding this experience is proving to be for me. "

Mentees also explain in the book all the benefits and the value received from their work relationship in business management.

The network of mentors in Madrid is undoubtedly a great initiative, and this book is of particular value in this regard, anyone interested in entrepreneurial issues cannot forget to read this book. This work has such an effect, that I dare to say, it is essential to the smooth functioning of the economy of our country.

Cholo Simeone, model of leader.

All business schools should include the example of Cholo Simeone when discussing business leadership.

A soccer team is a very special type of company where the usual problems of management are monstrous because of the unique nature of the stakes; shareholders, employees/players, clients/partners, supporters and public/media opinion. All with unique characteristics and high degree of sensitivity to the progress of the company/team.

The coach is definitely the hub of the whole business network, the undisputed leader, always criticized. And its importance is more momentous than in any other company.

When looking at the success story of the company Atletico de Madrid during the 2013/2014 season, the performance of their leader and the qualities developed by Cholo are an example of what a leader should be in any other type of business.

Objectives: One basic principle is not to start with aspirations to reach unattainable goals like winning the League Cup or the Champions League, but establish short-term objectives that can be renewed as they are reached.

Strategy: To think of every match as if it was the most important.

Motivation: Persuading the team that they are as good as any of the best players in the world and if they give their best, there is no rival they cannot compete with.

Team spirit: All players are equally important; there must not be untouchable divas. The team is the real star.

Sacrifice and courage: At the end of each match, make them understand that courage and sacrifice becomes invaluable when victory is achieved.

Enthusiasm and passion: Lead from a commanding position and live every match with the same enthusiasm and passion as the players. Always transmit confidence in attaining victory.

Reward: When all targets are met and success follows, the whole team enjoys it together with his leader.

Nobody doubts that Cholo Simeone is the architect of this Atleti team who just won the League and next Saturday will compete to win the Cup in the Champions League final. A great example of the role of a leader for any company that wants to succeed in their respective business area.

The imperfect leadership

My good friend Nuria Vilanova, CEO of Inforpress, the largest Spanish media consultant, writes in her book "Micropowers" about what she defines a flawed leadership.

I loved the explanation she gives of how that theory came to her: She says it was during a leadership course she was imparting at the IESE Business School, and the struggles she had when she tried to correct the shortcomings of the guidelines that were made according to the canons of the prestigious institution. "I tried to be ordered, follow routines, repeat processes, improve monitoring processes. I almost died. Until I realized how unhappy that made me and was losing my great advantage: the strength I have when I am involved in what I love doing, I felt as if I was loosing what I am good at: creativity, business acumen, sales and mobilization of talent. So I decided to invent a new theory: Imperfect leadership."

Nuria speaks from her experience of being a leader of a company she created from scratch; it now has more than 200 employees with offices in Spain, Portugal, Brazil, Colombia and Peru.
She knows what she's talking about and is convinced that one can only succeed with passion, doing what you like and developing your skills. One of her proposals is that "it is essential not to try hiding your personal limitations to your team", and to learn to "ask for help and create a group to compliment all those areas where we do not stand out".

In my own personal experience leading a successful advertising agency, I agree with Nuria that nobody is a perfect leader, and we all need to surround ourselves with the wisdom and qualities of others.

Nuria gives us three tips in her book to become the imperfect leader:

1) Know where your weaknesses are.

2) Be honest with your team about them.

3) Be humble and ask for help.

Sounds easy, but there's nothing more difficult than to recognize our shortcomings and let others know about them. Try it, and if you can be a good "Imperfect Leader", congratulations, because that's the way to be a great leader for real.

Speaking about leaders

If you're an Apple fan you can't miss the movie "Jobs" and probably you will enjoy it, provided Ashton Kutcher is not entirely up to the part, nor the script delves into the more interesting facets of the personality and work of Steve Jobs.

Like all geniuses, Jobs was a rare and antisocial type, not only was he dirty always barefoot, and smelling very bad and on the human level he had a despicable character. The film portrays, to some degree, his bad temper and behavior towards the people he was closest, but falls short when it comes to face reality, he himself speaks about it in his autobiography, a magnificent book written by Walter Isaacson, which reflects accurately all the important aspects of the life and work of the great character who was Steve Jobs.

I do not think that you should to read the book to try to understand the dark personality of the genius, but to better understand his work, to extract extremely useful professional lessons to become an entrepreneur.
And don't forget to see the magnificent speech Jobs gave at Stanford University in the graduation ceremony class of 2005. A real life lesson that goes far beyond the miseries tat Jobs had as a human being.

The attitude of the leader in front of the crisis

One of the most important things I have learned in my professional career is to weather bad news. As president of an advertising agency, with a staff of about seventy people, I had to get used to a host of daily calamities, not because the agency was bad, (fortunately it was almost always pretty good), but because when you manage a company you have to deal with the problems where others have exhausted their possibilities to solve them.

Staff problems, unbearable pressures from our Boston headquarters, creative people missing deadlines, executives being pressured by the customer, unpaid bills and dozens of other issues all equally important. Solving awkward problems and having to make immediate decisions is part of the salary of the leader, to show the way to others. You also have to be capable to support their dramas on your shoulders and be the person they turn to when they have exhausted their possibilities to solve problems, and always have a solution. You can never fail, because you are the last resort and everyone will accept the decisions that will affect the operations and future of the company, good or bad, because you're the boss.

Making decisions is never easy; everyone learns to develop his or her own system. In my case, I always expect the worst and start by analyzing the problem with calm, like a bag of tea soaking in my head; it could be a day, a few hours or a few minutes depending on the situation. I never make a decision in haste; I evaluate the worst consequences of the situation, and once I have assumed the worst, I'm prepared to make the decision I find most convenient.

In some cases it is possible to make decisions without pressure, like when we needed to start a new project or when the problems that may have an affect on us come from the outside and are not necessarily urgent. In such cases, and more than ever, we must be cautious and calculate all the parameters of the situation and imagine the worst consequences.

In my book "How to achieve success from failure to failure" I gave as an example my attitude towards the phenomenon that shook the business world in the late nineties, the Internet.

It is said that the light at the end of a tunnel does not always mean that the end is close; it may also be the light of a train ready to run us over. It is important to contemplate this possibility with confidence and make sure that you have a clear path if the train passes and move towards the exit walking down the side of the tunnel, close to the wall so not to be hit by the train.

Having the worst situations in mind is not a pessimistic approach to the problem; it helps you evaluate the situation so nothing catches us by surprise. Our decisions should not be taken lightly; the success of a good manager rests in making good decisions.

Praise of failure

Oscar Wilde said, "There are only two tragedies in life: one is not getting what one wants, and the other is getting it. It is one of my favorite quotes I give on my lectures, because I think it masterfully synthesizes the meaning of life, the constant pursuit of a goal that we really never achieve. But the greatness of our existence is that we will never fulfill our desires.

In the most prosaic level of our career, the goal is to get our aspirations, and when they are not met, they bring enormous frustration, a tragedy sometimes; but then they should be replaced immediately by a new goal, a new target that will allow us to continue in our path: the path that, whether paved with success or failure, gives meaning to our professional lives.

Antonio Machado wrote: "Wanderer, your footsteps are the road, and nothing more; wanderer, there is no road, the road is made by walking. The secret is to walk not necessarily getting anywhere, just keep walking. You have to understand failure as a fact of life, and you should never turn away from it. On the contrary, failure or our failures are the required goals in the way to success.

Ever since I can remember, failure has accompanied me; in school, on loving environments or in my professional field, failure has always been close to me, it's the spur I need to conquer my greatest obstacles. Obviously my case is not unique, failure also accompanies the lives of all human beings, because it is an inseparable aspect of our evolution.

Therefore, it is very important that we learn to live with it, to accept it as a partner in our journey through life and also to take advantage of it, obtaining juicy experiences for our personal development.

To fail is to grow stronger.

Failures are about accepting our limits and learn, a necessary and indispensable step to expand the road to success. Sometimes it is very difficult to recognize our failures, we usually blame others for our mistakes, we blame our bad luck, circumstances were not favorable to us and ultimately it was our fate. In this way we avoid absorbing failures and learn from them, and that's the worst mistake. If we ignore our own weaknesses we obstruct the way to develop our strengths.

Failure is a learning imperative.

Failure is not just a normal occurrence but is also good and necessary. When we are babies we have an infinite curiosity and an excessive urge to learn everything, but we cannot touch everything we would have wanted, to stand or express verbally our needs, we encounter failure again and again but nevertheless, that does not discourage us. To fail over and over again is a sort of constant stimulus and in the world failure is more constant and enthusiastic than a baby; to him failure is just a powerful stimulant. With failure he learns to improve his technique to get the things he or she wants, without it we could never evolve in any aspect of life.

A continuous chain of failures composes the learning period of a baby. However, it is the most fruitful period in the stage of a human life. Glenn Doman, the great pioneer in the field of brain development in children, says that most of our ability to learn happens between birth and six years, where our brain is like a sponge. We try to learn everything, take in everything, understand it all and naturally we fail again and again in our attempts. But ultimately, in a few years, we learn to walk upright, speak one or more languages, read, write and develop a thought process and in that period a baby is never discouraged by failure; on the contrary, it is the most suitable method to learn from our mistakes and reach our objectives.

In the world of adults, failure is manifested in all kinds of situations and activities. We fail when we try to establish relations of any kind with others, when we study in school or in college, when we try to find our first job and when we must make our own decisions. Failure is always with us, but we should not feel it's all over; a real loss is when you are unable to live with your failures.

Sometimes a failure is just a feeling.

We are overwhelmed by the task ahead, or the responsibility demanded from us, and if we allow the sense of failure to poorly conduct our life, it can lead us to a real loss.

It is important to distinguish between a concern and a failure, between the weight of responsibility and a failure, and between small setbacks and a failure. We only really fail when we get confused between failure and the above mentioned and in the end of a stage, we haven't achieved the objectives we set out to accomplish or come close to the expected results. Only absolute failure can be described as a failure. And if that happens to us, we should not complain in finding solace, but dig to find the enthusiasm to develop a new plan that will lead us to success. A plan that takes into consideration our previous failures and where we can analyze, point by point, all the causes that led us to fail in the previous attempt.

The secret of success.

Most people think that success has more to do with fate and luck than with daily effort. It is thought that being in the right place at the right time is enough; nothing can be further from the truth. Luck and chances are not enough to succeed. As Picasso pointed out, "Inspiration exists, but it has to find you working."

Work, work, work, that's one of the main keys to find success in anything. It is true that you should not miss opportunities, but its not enough to be surrounded by them if you are not willing to work hard to seize the moment. And it's not only hard work, there are millions of people who work hard and never achieve success.

There are any numbers of good examples in elite athletes who fail to materialize success. Every match for a football player, a tennis player, a golfer or even a lecture, are opportunities to achieve success. Every time a bullfighter that enters the ring or athletes in the Olympic games are surrounded with all the elements to succeed but statistics show that there are more gray days than shiny moments. For every moment of triumph there are many others of defeat and failure. However, the real winner, which really becomes a star in his or her own right, is the one who does not succumb to failure and again and again learns from his mistakes and trains harder without being discouraged by defeat, without crumbling in the face of adversity. Work hard and learn to overcome failures: therein lies the secret of success.

Less is always more

Last weekend I read a report in one of the Sunday supplements of a newspaper, that the great British photographer David Bailey took part of an exhibition organized by the National Portrait Gallery in London, with the title "Bailey's Stardust", a collection of over 250 of his photographs, some of them unpublished, like the portrait of model Kate Moss, that illustrates the article.

Jessica Nieto, the journalist who wrote the article, says that sincerity is the word that best defines the photographs of Bailey. And if David were a color, it would be black and white, the trademark of all his work. There is a small statement in the article from the photographer himself: "I always look for simplicity".

The article made me remember my own experience with David who received the OBE (Order of the British Empire) in 2001, and I had the honor of meeting him in the late 70s when he was at the height of his glorious career and after divorcing the second of his four wives, the actress Catherine Deneuve, it certainly contributed to give exposure to his work as a photographer.

When I was the creative director of the Foote, Cone & Belding agency, I hired David Bailey to direct a TV commercial for a shampoo called Born of the Earth, from the Gillette Company. David not only directed the spot, but also, and not surprisingly, was responsible for the photography.

We shot the spot in the greenhouse of a magnificent house in Somosaguas, where, a in a beautiful bathroom, a model was washing her hair. For the final product shot, David placed on a marble surface several hair related tools, clothing products, and a pearl brush, ribbons of many colors, a silver box and some thing else I can't remember.
He filmed a close up with all the elements around the shampoo bottle. And then he would remove one element every time a new plane was shot, until only one remained on the bare marble slab.

He then explained to me that he loved the simplicity, and that he liked to see how each item would behave by removing the presence of the most powerful product, and it was important to continue that process, because the things he was removing gave us information on the most favorable viewing angle for the product shot.

Lifehacking: the art of doing nothing

A few days ago I read in El País newspaper an interesting article written by Stanford University Professor, Evgeny Morozov on the phenomenon of life hacking, one of the buzzwords today in Silicon Valley.

At first, the term was defined as the smartest way to use technology to increase the productivity of individuals. However, that interpretation has now given a180 degree turn, it now means the use of technology to work less and have more leisure time.

In Morozov's book *"The 4 hour workweek"*, a famous Timothy Ferriss's bestseller, widely develops the philosophy behind the mentioned life hacking approach: use technology not to be more entangled in work most our time, but quite the opposite.

It is much less the use of technological tools, but to use them better, like not spending the whole day attached to a tablet or on a Smartphone downloading useless platitudes and applications, but how you apply all the technological advantages to give you time off.

Another neuroscience specialist, Andrew Smart, said that according to the latest findings, our brains, while at rest is doing a lot of work, and that *"spending time doing nothing is absolutely necessary to fully develop our mental faculties and addressing new and original perspectives. To innovate, therefore, it is absolutely necessary to learn to be idle."*

I agree with Ferriss and Smart, because I have always known that the trick is to think and to do just that, stop our constant activity. The continuous and relentless effort if managers and business leaders, sometimes prevents them to think properly and end up limiting their capacity to innovate and develop, making them ineffective.

You must try to forget your technological tools for several hours in a day and spend time thinking and enjoy leisure time. Suddenly you'll see how everything starts to become clearer and more defined, in your life and in your work, but especially in your creativity.

Latin America

In the mid 90s I was president of a group of independent European advertising agencies called MAPP. Every six months, the leaders of each agency met in one of the member countries. On one occasion, in the city of Lyon, we present a common project to a group of French journalists. And together with our German, Swedish, English, Italian and French colleagues, we explained to the audience our vision of the world of advertising and business.

After the event, I was interviewed by the French television, and at the end of the interview, the French journalist told me: *"I have listened carefully to all interventions. And my final conclusion is that you Spaniards are the only ones who have something interesting to say. I sincerely believe that Spain is the only alive country in Europe".*

Today I have the same impression the French journalist had but in regards of Latin America, I think it's the only place where Spanish-speaking people are still alive.

In my capacity as a lecturer, I travel very often to the Americas; Chile, Colombia, Costa Rica and the Dominican Republic have been some of my recent destinations. And I had the same feeling everywhere. While we here complain about the crisis and the lack of opportunities, in Latin America they work with enthusiasm to innovate and develop.

Certainly our living standards, despite our economic situation, are not comparable. However, they feel more alive than us. There are also many problems of corruption and suffer the inefficiency of some of their government leaders, but have never perceived themselves as an exhausted project.

They attend conferences with enthusiasm and eager to learn, and strive to achieve the best for their careers. They are a true example of vitality and enthusiasm, a true example to follow in these sad days for all of us in Spain.

Looking for trends? Go to Japan

I do not remember if it was the poet Gabriel Celaya or Gabriel Otero who wrote many years ago: *"We have to go to China to Orient us",* it was proven to be a premonition prodigy. The future is in the east and we have to go there for guidance. China is still in the boiling period and although the changes are dizzying, they still take some years to contemplate their future in all its glory. Japan, however, has already been setting the pace of modernity in many ways.

I was in Japan for the first time in 1991. It was a quick sightseeing tour of three of the most iconic cities: Osaka, Kyoto and Tokyo, they all dazzled me with their own particular style. I came back to visit the same cities and a few others with a more professional stare concentrating on publicity, classical art, fashion, luxury shopping and new trends for my work as a strategic consultant I found everything in abundance.

Traffic jams are still the same, especially in Tokyo, a city jammed up together where buildings are clustered on top of each other, without any concession to the order or the landscape. Access roads to the city are superimposed on each other to form four storey avenues crammed with cars without movement. Peak hours in Spain are nothing compared to that overwhelming urban reality. However, in the middle of all that chaos, there is harmony of life and beauty. Of course a different type harmony than ours, with that particular nature of the Japanese to never look directly into your eyes.

Nothing in the city is subordinated to our unidirectional geometry, including relationships with people. The doors of the gardens are never aligned with the doors of the houses. To access the interior of an ultramodern building we have to make a detour following the contours of a pond, and sit on meditation in the oldest Zen garden known fixing our gaze on seventeen asymmetric stones, resting on a bed of sand.

The Japanese are a rare bunch with an inordinate fondness for neon lights and karaoke. The shopping streets of any major Japanese city is like a gigantic Times Square, where plasma screens surely compete with the deafening noise of the pachinkos, where hundreds of players are in communion with an infernal machine that works with steel balls. It's like being in a video game where music, images and high decibels are part of a dizzying montage, which stuns the senses.

Advertising is everywhere. On the streets, in the subway, in the shopping centers and inside buildings, where the lower floors are intertwined with each other forming large underground avenues full of shops, cafeterias, fast food restaurants, and people. Thousands of people walking fast without looking, but seen through the eyes of Orwell's Big Brother plasma screens, like in the version Ridley Scott did for Apple's Macintosh launch spot in 1984. That is, from the ubiquitous screens.

Street screens are used for everything from conventional advertising spots, with or without audio often with a soundtrack connected via Bluetooth to your mobile phone, video clips of popular singers and to even offer a free show to look at oneself while crossing, accompanied by thousands of people, the busiest street in the world, where six crosswalks converge with green lights all at the same time in Osaka, making the act of crossing the crowded street into a perfectly synchronized ballet.

Unlike Spaniards, the Japanese are predictable, structured and very disciplined, they are proud of that fact and display it in every corner of the land, where everything is designed to their own measure, without any concession to the Western world, despite appearances. For example, in Japan almost nobody speaks English, or indeed any other language other than Japanese, they don't even bother to make it easy to the visitor by writing in Latin characters the most essential texts.

There are many subway stations where you never know where you are, and many restaurants where you cannot eat if you do not understand the alphabet.

They do not think in terms of tourism, and the truth is that they are very few Western tourists walking their crowded streets, where smoking is prohibited, you can only smoke in some specific areas where smoke blowers huddle before the critical gaze of their neighbors, many of them with protective by masks.

In every city, sidewalks have a yellow line in relief to indicate the blind where to walk, where to cross and where to enter the subway or buildings; a sound also helps them locate elevators or escalators. In the subway, next to the famous pushers with white gloves, that push people into wagons at peak hours before the doors close without harming anyone, we can also see pink wagons for the exclusive use of women, where they will be safe from any possible sexual abuse. Before they did suffered sexual assaults, but being as submissive as they are they did not dare to protest.

Taxi drivers wear suits and ties and most often white gloves. Their vehicles are spacious, spotless and the doors open and close automatically when you approach them. Japanese drivers will never cheat on the fair and you do not have to tip them. Tipping is not customary anywhere in Japan, much less an obligation; we were extraordinarily grateful for that. The service is always fast and flawless, also in hotels and restaurants, where you can frequently find a bell on each table to call the waiter without having to raise your voice or make hand gestures.

There is also modernity and modernism in the shining and dazzling architecture everywhere to satisfy our sense of awe, particularly the work of some great architects such as Tadao Ando. I must also point out to the beautiful architecture of luxury shops, a powerful communication weapon fashionable among the major brands. Today, New York is no longer the major showcase for international luxury, Tokyo is the best showcase to be seen, and all the big brands know it. Almost all of them: Dior, Hermes, Chloe, Prada or Tods have their temples in the district of Ginzha, or at the more fashionable Omotesando. Luxury brands know that these buildings are the flagships for this type of personality, nothing to do with a conventional store, they are true masterpieces of over ten stories high, where they project to the world their image and strength. An image that, as in the case of Dior, can be

seen reproduced in the design of hundreds of stores located in shopping centers around the world.
Definitely a smart marketing strategy developed by one of the luxury brands that have successfully marketed their image on clothing, accessories, cosmetics or perfumes over the last 50 years.

Japan is the place that makes the difference, and if you want an insight into the 21'st century, you should focus your attention on Japan.
A magical place where you can discover the secret of an ancient culture and get a glimpse of the mysteries of the near future that will soon be here with us.
Discipline and modernity are two unique features found everywhere. Modernity is present in the most intimate places, like in the mixture of toilette and bidet, so practical, with trickles of water directed to strategic spots. Or in the fierce fashion wore by generally petite women, with bowed legs, no ass or hips, that dare to wear mini skirts, high boots, mid-calf leggings, mini shorts, or open back shorts. A real trendsetting horror, our women will look much better than the Japanese.

www.ingramcontent.com/pod-product-compliance
Lightning Source LLC
Chambersburg PA
CBHW071436180526
45170CB00001B/368